The Cathars

Other books by Sean Martin

The Black Death
Alchemy and Alchemists
The Knights Templar
The Gnostics

Andrei Tarkovsky
New Waves in Cinema

As contributor

Through the Mirror:
Reflections on the Films of Andrei Tarkovsky
Temple Antiquities: The Templar Papers II
Music for Another World
Rocket Science

The Cathars

SEAN MARTIN

POCKET ESSENTIALS

This edition published in 2014
by Pocket Essentials,
an imprint of Oldcastle Books,
PO Box 394, Harpenden,
Herts, AL5 1XJ, UK

Reprinted 2015

A CIP catalogue record for this book is available from the British Library.

ISBN 978-1-84344-336-0 (print)
978-1-84344-416-9 (epub)
978-1-84344-417-6 (kindle)
978-1-84344-418-3 (pdf)

Typeset by Avocet Typeset, Somerton, Somerset
Printed and bound in Great Britain by CPI Group (UK) Ltd, Croydon, CR0 4YY

For all the Good Christians, past and present

and

In Memory of My Father,
whose feet tread the lost aeons

Acknowledgements

I would like to thank Ion Mills, for bearing with me during the writing of this book; my sister Lois, for her advice; Nick Harding, for the usual lending of tomes and camaraderie; and fellow *credente* Adso Brown.

A Note on the Second Edition

For this edition, I have corrected a number of errors in the text and updated the bibliography. I would like to thank Dr Cyril Edwards for clarifying certain matters regarding Germanic Grail literature. The final chapter has received a revamp, in order to add some clarity to the bewildering array of myths surrounding the Cathars.

Throughout human history, believers have waged war against one another. Gnostics and mystics have not. People are only too prepared to kill on behalf of a theology or a faith. They are less disposed to do so on behalf of knowledge. Those prepared to kill for faith will therefore have a vested interest in stifling the voice of knowledge.

Michael Baigent and Richard Leigh,
The Inquisition

Bishop Fulk, asking a knight why he did not expel heretics, received the classic answer: 'We cannot. We have been reared in their midst. We have relatives among them and we see them living lives of perfection.'

Malcolm Lambert,
The Cathars

Salvation is better achieved in the faith of these men called heretics than in any other faith.

Anonymous French peasant, quoted in
Emmanuel Le Roy Ladurie, *Montaillou*

Contents

Prologue
Béziers

It was the Feast Day of St Mary Magdalene, 22 July 1209, and an all-out massacre had not been planned.

A French army from the north, under the leadership of the Papal legate Arnold Amaury, was camped outside the town of Béziers in the Languedoc. Recently arrived from a month-long march down the valley of the River Rhône, the army's mission was to demand that the town elders hand over the 222 Cathars – less than 10 per cent of the town's population[1] – that they were known to be harbouring. The elders refused. That they did so says as much for the power of the Cathar faith as it does for the complicated political situation in the south in which the Cathars had been able to flourish.

The Cathars had come to prominence in the Languedoc some fifty years previously and were, by the beginning of the thirteenth century, virtually the dominant religion in the Languedoc. Unlike the majority of the Catholic clergy of the time, the Cathars were conspicuously virtuous, living lives of apostolic poverty and simplicity. This in itself would have been enough to get the sect branded as heretics, as happened to the Lyons-based group, the Waldensians.[2] But what set the Cathars apart from the Waldensians was their belief in not one god, but two. According to Cathar theology, there were two eternal principles, good and evil, with the world being under the sway of the latter. They were also implacably hostile to the Church of Rome, which they denounced vehemently as the Church of Satan.

The Cathars were not the only ones to oppose Rome: most of the south of what we would today call France was fiercely independent, and regarded both the northern army and the Papal agents as foreign invaders. It was therefore unthinkable that the Cathars, fellow southerners, could be handed over to opposition. The enemy was not heresy, but anyone who challenged the authority and autonomy of the local nobility, the powerful counts and viscounts of Toulouse, Foix and Carcassonne.

The combination of heresy and politics was a combustible one, however, and Pope Innocent III (1198–1216) saw sufficient grounds to call for a Crusade. The west had been launching Crusades with varying degrees of success ever since 1095, but they had all been directed against the Muslims. Under Innocent's pontificate, that began to change. The Fourth Crusade, launched in 1202, did not bode well for the heretics and nobles of the Languedoc: although aimed at the Holy Land, the Crusaders veered wildly off target in the spring of 1204 and sacked the fellow Christian city of Constantinople. The campaign called against the Cathars was different: it would be the first Crusade to be conducted within the west, against people who were fellow countrymen and women.

Arnold Amaury called for a meeting with his generals. It was clear that the heretics were not going to be given up without a fight. While the meeting was going on, a fracas broke out between a small band of Crusaders and a group on the walls of the town. Insults were exchanged. In a rash move, the defenders opened the gates and a small group of men from Béziers ventured out to teach the Crusaders some manners. They swiftly dealt with the northerners, but the news quickly spread that the gate was open. Crusaders poured into the town. Word got back to Arnold Amaury. What should they do? How would they recognise Cathars from Catholics? The Papal legate, paraphrasing 2 Timothy,[3] uttered the notorious command: 'Kill them all. God will recognise his own.'

In the ensuing bloodbath of 'abattoir Christianity',[4] approximately 8,000 or 9,000 innocent people were butchered. (The traditional figure of between 15,000 to 20,000 victims – claimed by pro-crusade apologists – is now thought to be too high; the population of Béziers in 1209 was probably less than 15,000.) Even women and children taking refuge in the Cathedral of St Nazaire were not spared: the cathedral was torched, and anyone caught fleeing was put to the sword. By the evening, rivers of blood coursed through the streets of Béziers. Churches and houses smouldered. Once they had finished killing, the Crusaders looted what was left.

The Albigensian Crusade, as it came to be known, had begun. Unlike the Fourth Crusade, however, it had gone out of control at the very beginning. The atrocities of Béziers would have confirmed to Cathars everywhere their belief that they alone were God's elect, and that the world was indeed evil.

1

Heresy and Orthodoxy

Catharism was the most popular heresy of the Middle Ages. Indeed, such was its success that the Catholic Church and its apologists referred to it as the Great Heresy. As the twelfth century turned into the thirteenth, it was at its zenith: Cathars could be found from Aragon to Flanders, from Naples to the Languedoc. Its equivalent of priests, the Perfect, lived lives so conspicuously virtuous that even their enemies had to proclaim that they were indeed holy and good people. The Cathars found widespread support from all areas of society, from kings and counts to carpenters and weavers. Women, never welcomed by the Church, became Cathars knowing they could earn respect and actively participate in the faith. Needless to say, this mixture of women, virtue and apostolic poverty — to say nothing of the Cathar church's popularity — did not sit well with Rome. But nor did Rome sit well with the Cathars, who believed that the Church had, in its pursuit of worldly power, betrayed Christ's message.

That Catholicism would move against the Cathars was hardly surprising; indeed, in some areas in the south of France, Cathars were more numerous than Catholics. What shocked contemporaries was not that the Pope ordered a Crusade to put the heresy down, but that the Crusaders committed atrocities of such magnitude that they are still echoing down the centuries. In the Languedoc, these crimes have never really been forgotten.

Strangely, for all its popularity, the exact origins of Catharism are unknown. It emerged at a time when the Church, and Europe as a whole, was undergoing enormous changes prior to emerging into the so-called Renaissance of the twelfth century. Although it is difficult to imagine the scale of atrocities such as Béziers, we can go some way to understanding the mindset of the Cathars' persecutors by studying the history of the Church and how heresy emerged from it. Moreover, a study of the history of the dualist heresy – essentially, the belief that the devil is as powerful as God, to which Catharism belongs – will help to set things in perspective. Like Catharism, Dualism has murky beginnings.

Dualism

Dualism existed before Christianity, and may even be older than recorded history itself. The term was first coined in 1700 by the English Orientalist, Thomas Hyde, to describe any religious system which held that God and the devil were two opposing, coeternal principles.[5] The meaning of the term evolved to include any system that revolved around a central, binary pairing (such as the mind/body split in the philosophy of Descartes, or the immortal soul/mortal body in that of Plato). Dualist strands exist in one form or another in all major religions, whether monotheistic (acknowledging one god, such as Islam, Judaism and Christianity), polytheistic (acknowledging many gods, such as Shintoism, some forms of Wicca or the pantheon of classical Greece), or monistic (acknowledging that everything – the Divine, matter and humanity – is of one and the same essential substance, such as certain schools of Hinduism, Buddhism, Taoism and Pantheism). For example, fundamentalist Christianity has a pronounced dualist slant in that it sees many things in the world – rock music, drugs, New Age philosophies, Hollywood blockbusters – as being the work of the devil. Likewise, extremist Islamic groups see non-Muslims as either essentially asleep to the truth, or actively engaged in undermining the religion of the Prophet. In both cases, an 'us and them' mentality prevails, from which there is only one escape route (belief in Jesus and Mohammed respectively).

Despite these varying levels of Dualism in the different faiths of the world, religious Dualism proper stands apart in positing the notion of the two opposing principles of good and evil. Within the dualist tradition itself, there are generally held to be two schools of thought: absolute, or radical, Dualism; and mitigated, or monarchian, Dualism. The Italian historian of religions, Ugo Bianchi, identified three distinct features of Dualism:

1) Absolute Dualism regards the two principles of good and evil as coeternal and equal, whereas mitigated Dualism regards the evil principle as a secondary, lesser power to the good principle.
2) Absolute Dualism sees the two principles as locked in combat for all eternity, and, in many schools, regards time as cyclical (many absolute dualists, therefore, tend to believe in reincarnation), whilst mitigated Dualism sees historical time

as being finite; at the end of time, the evil principle will be defeated by the good.

3) Absolute Dualism sees the material world as intrinsically evil, but mitigated Dualism regards creation as essentially good.[6]

The Good Religion

Zoroastrianism is usually held to be the first major world religion to espouse a dualistic view of the world. However, the Dualism present in ancient Egyptian religion predates Zoroastrianism by some centuries, if not a millennium (the exact dates of the founding of Zoroastrianism being unknown). Polarities – such as that of light and dark – are frequently found in ancient Egyptian religious thought, perhaps the best known of them being the opposition of Horus (sometimes Osiris) and Seth. In the various versions of the myth that have survived, the two gods are portrayed as being constantly at war with one another, with Seth never being able to destroy Horus (despite blinding him in one eye), but who himself is never quite annihilated either. They were known variously as 'the two gods', 'the two brothers' and 'the two fighters'. Although they weren't originally seen as good (Horus) versus evil (Seth), Seth developed trickster-type attributes and was gradually demonised until his name was virtually anathema in Egyptian religious rituals and was effectively banished from the Egyptian pantheon.

As Seth was gradually becoming depicted in ever darker colours, a dualist system that posited good against evil from its very outset was emerging in Persia. The prophet Zoroaster (also known as Zarathustra) was a great Persian religious reformer who founded what he called the Good Religion, or Zoroastrianism. The dates of his mission are unclear, and Zoroaster has been placed in various epochs, from 1700–1400 BC to 1400–1000 BC or 1000–600 BC. Current research tends to suggest the middle dates, making Zoroastrianism the world's oldest revealed religion, a religion that 'has probably had more influence on mankind, directly and indirectly, than any other single faith.'[7] Zoroaster was 'the first to teach the doctrines of an individual judgment, heaven and hell, the future resurrection of the body, the general Last Judgment, and life everlasting for the reunited soul and body.'[8] All of these ideas were to influence Judaism, Christianity and Islam. Yet where Zoroastrianism differs from these later religions is in its treatment of evil. In its traditional form, the faith holds that there is one good god, Ahura Mazda (the name means Wise Lord), under whom are the two equal twin forces of Spenta Mainyu (the beneficent or holy spirit) and Angra Mainyu (the hostile or destructive spirit). Although Ahura Mazda's creation is good, the source of all evil within it is caused by Angra Mainyu, who is destined to be overcome at the end of historical time, at which point eternity will begin.

Classical Zoroastrianism, however, underwent changes as the fortunes of the Persian Empire rose and fell. Over time, Ahura Mazda became identified with Spenta Mainyu, reducing the original trinity to a binary pairing. The names of the Wise Lord and his adversary also underwent transformation, being contracted to Ohrmazd and Ahriman respectively. By the time of the Achaemenid Dynasty (550–330 BC), Ahriman was no longer seen as being created by, and inferior to, Ohrmazd, but was now regarded as his equal.[9]

The World, the Flesh and the Devil

Zoroastrianism, in all its forms, regards the world as a battleground between the forces of good and evil, and each individual is expected to make their own choice as to which side to be on. This, together with the idea of the two principles, would later resurface in Catharism. Several other concepts that developed before the Christian era would also help to shape the heresy, namely the split between the body and the soul, and the figure of the Judeo-Christian equivalent of Ahriman, Satan.

The body/soul split, although perhaps today synonymous with Descartes[10] and modern empirical science, seems to have first emerged with the cult of Orpheus in the sixth century BC, which came to play an important part in the religious life of ancient Greece. Orphism contained elements of Dualism within it, as the legendary figure of Orpheus was said to be either the son of Apollo or the Thracian king Oeagres, who was of the dynasty founded by Dionysus. Apollo, the god of order and reason, traditionally stood opposite Dionysus, the god of intoxication and ecstasy, but in Orphism, as in later Zoroastrianism, neither god prevails over the other. Unlike Zoroastrianism, however, which regards the body as the material vehicle of the soul, Orphism regarded the soul as divine and immortal, while the body was its evil, mortal prison for the duration of its earthly existence. The origins of this belief derive from the story of the child Dionysus: as the son of Zeus, the boy incurred the jealousy of the Titans, the race of elder gods that Zeus had overthrown. The Titans tempted the child with a mirror, and while he was studying his own reflection, the Titans killed and dismembered the boy.[11] Although Dionysus is later resurrected, Zeus destroys the Titans with a salvo of thunderbolts, and it is from the remains of the elder gods that humankind is born. The physical body was held to be made of Titanic material, and therefore evil, while the soul was formed of divine Dionysian material. Orphism developed practices whose focus was the fate of the soul in the afterlife, and the Orphic initiate hoped that, by following these practices, their soul would be granted salvation in the next world and released from the bonds of matter and the cycle of death and rebirth.

Satan was originally an accusing angel in Hebrew thought,[12] but had the good fortune, like Ahriman before him, to be promoted. In the Book of Job, the earliest Old Testament book in which he has a prominent role,[13] Satan is one of the 'sons of God' (Job 1.6) who serve God in heaven. God asks Satan for a progress report on what he has been up to of late. Satan replies 'I have been walking here and there, roaming around the earth' (Job 1.7). God asks Satan if he has noticed the devout Job, describing him as His most faithful servant. Satan wonders if Job would still serve God if he, Job, had everything taken away from him. God concedes the point, and lets Satan descend to Earth to begin testing Job.

In a rapid sequence of calamities that could rightly be called Old Testament in their severity, Job has his donkeys stolen by Sabeans (Job 1.15), his sheep (and attendant shepherds) are suddenly struck by lightning and killed a verse later, while, in verse seventeen, Chaldeans make off with his camels. Before Job has time to react, another breathless servant comes running with news even worse: a storm has destroyed the house that Job's children were feasting in; all were killed. Job tears his clothes in grief, shaves his head and, from a position face down on the floor, praises the Lord for taking that which He had originally given.

Satan returns to heaven, and God points out to him that, despite the fact that Satan has done his worst to Job, Job's faith is unshaken. God feels that He has won the toss, but Satan, not to be outdone by his employer, asks God if Job's faith will be as strong if his body were to be attacked. Once more, God allows Satan to test Job, on the condition that he doesn't kill the poor man. This time, Satan causes sores to break out all over Job's body. Rather than seek sound medical advice, Job decides to scrape at his sores with a piece of broken pottery. Once again, Job rejoices in his suffering, and Satan retires, temporarily, from the narrative.

Satan plays the role of a trickster in the Book of Job, albeit one of a rather cruel bent. There is no doubt that he is still, essentially, a heavenly servant of some kind: if Satan is not actually doing God's bidding, then at least God seems content to let Satan get up to his tricks in the earthly realm. It is not until the Second Book of Chronicles, written sometime towards the close of the Achaemenid period (which ended in 330 BC), that Satan steps out from the shadow of the Almighty to become a force set firmly against God and His creation. He – Satan – does so in a rather interesting way, as he plays the role once taken by God Himself in an earlier telling of the story.[14] The story in question is of the census of the tribes of Israel, first recounted in the Second Book of Samuel, Chapter 24: the Lord, being angry yet again with Israel, forces David to number her peoples. David's army – who are to do the actual counting – are none too happy, but comply with their king's command. After nine months and twenty days, in which they have been all over Israel, they return to Jerusalem, the census complete. At this point, David has a crisis of conscience, and tells God that he feels that the census has been a terrible sin. Unfortunately for David and the people of Israel, God agrees. He gives David three choices to punish the sin: three years of famine;[15] three months of running away from his enemies; or three days of pestilence throughout the land. David is unable to decide, and casts himself at the mercy of his Lord. His Lord, however, is not at His most merciful, and smites the land with three days' plague, in which 70,000 Israelites perish. When the story is retold in Second Chronicles, however, it is Satan, not God, who urges David to take the census. It makes no difference: the results are, for the unfortunate Israelites, the same.

Quite why Satan went from being an accusing angel to emerging – around the end of the Achaemenid period – as the adversary of both God and Man, is still something of a mystery. One possible explanation for this change is linked with the situation in Israel after the Babylonish Captivity ended. It has been suggested[16] that, when the exiled tribes returned home, friction was generated between them and the tribes who had stayed; the exiles felt that it was they who were the true children of God, for they had remained true to the Torah and had suffered the punishment of exile to prove it. Matters came to a head in 168 BC, when the Seleucid ruler of Israel, King Antiochus Epiphanes, embarked on an anti-Semitic purge. Rebellion quickly spread, and when Antiochus's forces were defeated, it was the hardline descendants of the former exiles who gained control of the Temple. To them, the likes of the liberal pro-Hellenic Hasmonean dynasty were as much the enemy as the Seleucids, and it was perhaps these ongoing tensions within

Israel that led to Satan, formerly one of God's angels, becoming anathematised in the same way that the hardliners were excoriating the Hasmoneans for, as they saw it, their treachery and betrayal.

Essenes, Gnostics and the First Christians

If Dualism has beginnings that are obscured by the mists of time, then the origins of Christianity itself are likewise semi-obscured by the passage of the centuries. The Cathars claimed descent from early Christianity, before the Roman Church became the religion's dominant form. Roman rule of Israel – which began in 63 BC – was facing increasing resistance from various groups within Israel. Most notable among them were the Essenes, a radical Jewish group based in the caves of Qumran overlooking the Dead Sea. It has been suggested by various writers that both John the Baptist and Jesus himself were at one time members of the Dead Sea community before beginning their respective ministries. While this is debatable, it is known that the Essenes sought to establish a new covenant with God, as they believed that Israel's sins had all but invalidated the old covenant (given by God to Abraham). According to Roman historians like Josephus and Philo, the Essenes were divided between those who had taken full vows – which involved living at Qumran and adhering to a strict life of celibacy, prayer and ritual – and those who were associate members who, while Believers, lived in towns, plied ordinary trades and married. The Cathars – like their immediate forebears, the Bogomils – would also structure their church in this way.

In further foreshadowings of Catharism, the Essenes'

worldview was essentially dualist, in that they saw the world as the battleground between the forces of heaven and hell, and that man himself is the microcosm of this war: 'the spirits of truth and falsehood struggle within the human heart... According to his share in truth and right, thus a man hates lies; and according to his share in the lot of deceit, thus he hates the truth.'[17] They also insisted that what mattered was not one's ethnic origin – be it Jewish or Gentile – but one's morality: only the pure of heart would be saved.

While the Essenes may have been an influence on some of the earliest Christian communities, they did not influence all of them. Before the Church established what was and wasn't acceptable in the Christian faith at the First Council of Nicaea in the early fourth century, Christianity was a mixed bag of beliefs and practices. When the Cathars claimed that they were descended from the first Christians, they probably had in mind the sort of simple Christianity practised by the Apostles, and were certainly implying that they were part of the chain of true Christianity that thrived before the Council of Nicaea, which not only defined what constituted orthodox Christianity, but also, in doing so, defined what was heresy, and many of the early Christian groups ended up in the latter camp. To understand how this came to be so, we need to consider the fractious political situation in both Israel and the nascent Church in the first century.

Immediately during and after Jesus's ministry (which probably occurred between the mid twenties and mid thirties AD), his followers were a minority persecuted by both the Romans and the Pharisees alike. There is continuing controversy as to who was Jesus's successor in the movement. Peter is traditionally seen as the Rock upon which the Church was built,[18] and from whom the Roman Catholic Church claims descent, holding Peter as the first Pope. However, this is where problems set in. It has been argued[19] that Jesus's brother James, known as James the Greater, was the head of the first post-Crucifixion Christian community in Jerusalem, and it is thought that James's followers clashed with Christianity's most fervent missionary, St Paul. This becomes all the more important when one recalls that Paul's ideas played a large part – if not the largest – in forming the theology on which the Christian faith is based. And yet Paul remains a controversial figure: nowhere does he actually quote Jesus's words, and his letters – which form the largest part of the New Testament – are frequently addressed to other Christian communities clarifying points of doctrine or urging them to toe the line. Had early Christianity been a unified whole, there would have been no need for such letters. It would not be going too far to say that 'Paul, and not Jesus, was… the Founder of Christianity',[20] and therein lie the origins of Christian heresy: 'Paul is, in effect, the first "Christian" heretic, and his teachings – which became the foundation of later Christianity – are a flagrant deviation from the "original" or "pure" form.'[21] He is the 'first corrupter of the doctrines of Jesus',[22] as he never quotes from what Jesus himself actually taught. Jesus preached the Sermon on the Mount, Paul preached Christ Crucified; there is a big difference.

The Jewish Revolt of 66 AD effectively ended the Jerusalem church of James, while the Christianity of Paul, who was probably dead or dying in a cell in Rome at the time, would continue to grow. However, Pauline Christianity faced further challenges from the various unorthodox groups that sprang up in the three centuries before the Council of Nicaea sat. Certain of the groups developed the Dualism of the Essenes, and stressed the importance of *gnosis*, or direct experiential knowledge of the divine, and for that reason they are generally known as the Gnostics. Although there is a bewildering number of Gnostic schools of thought, each with their own, often complicated cosmologies, many of them did share the view that the world was created by an evil demiurge. Thus they are mitigated, or anti-cosmic, dualists. Perhaps the most important Gnostic school was that founded by Marcion in the mid-second century AD. Marcion proposed the existence of two gods: the true god, and the false god, the creator of the material world and the god of the Old Testament. Marcionites rejected the world and were rigorous ascetics. The emerging Roman Church recoiled in horror, and branded Marcion a heretic.

Aside from the idea of the two gods and the asceticism, another Gnostic idea would later reappear in Catharism, that of Christ as an apparition, not a flesh and blood human being. Many Gnostics saw Jesus's Passion and Resurrection as essentially ghostly, without any human suffering involved. This idea became known as Docetism, and was pronounced heretical. However, Catharism was to differ from many Gnostic schools of thought in its stress upon the way to salvation being only through the ministrations of the Perfect — rather than by direct *gnosis* on the part of the Believer. In doing so, Catharism would ironically mirror Catholicism, which claimed that the only way to salvation was through the intervention of its priests.

The Council of Nicaea

The course of western civilisation changed forever on 28 October 312, when the Roman Emperor Constantine the Great (306–37) achieved a decisive victory over his brother-in-law Maxentius at the Battle of Milvian Bridge, just outside Rome. The two men had been engaged in a power struggle since Constantine's accession, and at Milvian Bridge, matters came to a head. The night before the battle, however, things did not look good for Constantine. His men were outnumbered by 4:1, and defeat seemed likely. As evening drew on, Constantine saw the Greek letters *X P* ('Chi-Rho', the first two letters of the word 'Christ') suddenly appear on the setting sun together with a cross and the motto *In Hoc Signo Vinces* – 'in this sign you will conquer'. Constantine saw it as an omen, and ordered the cross be painted on his soldiers' shields. When he won an outright victory the next day, Constantine put the success down to the god of the Christians, converted to the faith and issued the Edict of Milan, which ordered an end to religious persecution across the empire.[23]

As soon as Christianity began to flourish with its new-found status, there were problems. Arianism, in particular, was proving to be controversial, with its view that God the Father and Christ the Son were two distinct entities, with Christ being seen as inferior to God. To settle the matter, Constantine convened the Council of Nicaea, whose opening session began on 20 May 325. In the two months that the Council sat, the 300 or so Church fathers gathered at Nicaea debated a number of topics, including the fixing of the date of Easter, but by far the most important issue was Arianism. In an attempt to establish

28

an orthodox position on Christ's divine nature, the Nicene Creed was promulgated on 19 June, which drew the battle lines between the orthodox and everyone else. Belief in the tenets of the Creed were central to orthodoxy. They included belief in 'God, the Father... maker of heaven and earth', in Christ 'the only Son of God... eternally begotten of the Father, true God from true God, begotten, not made, one in Being with the Father', who 'was born of the Virgin Mary and became man. For our sake he was crucified under Pontius Pilate; he suffered, died, and was buried. On the third day he rose again in fulfilment of the Scriptures.' Christ's flock was to be ministered unto solely by 'one holy catholic and apostolic Church.'[24] The key issue of Christ's divinity, and his being 'one in Being with the Father' was settled by vote. The Arians lost and were declared heretics. The Church was sending out a clear message: they were the only means by which one could achieve salvation.

Interestingly, one of the lesser matters that the Council of Nicaea dealt with – alongside what to do with zealots who had castrated themselves – was whether to welcome a strongly ascetic group back to the Church which had proclaimed strongly against Christians whose faith had lapsed, sometimes under torture. This group was known as the Cathars, or pure ones, from the Greek *katharoi*. Although this sect was not dualist and almost certainly had nothing to do with the mediaeval Cathars,[25] it is tempting to see their fate as an ominous precursor of what was to come: the Nicaean Cathars were denounced and declared heretics, and the cult died out altogether in the fifth century.

Manichaeism and Other Dualist Heresies

Although the religious ferment in the early centuries of the common era produced a welter of groups whose positions in relation to orthodoxy were to be defined, whether they liked it or not, by the Council of Nicaea, one new religion emerged during this time which was subsequently to put the Church into veritable palpitations at its very mention: Manichaeism. Manichaeism was founded by the Persian prophet Mani (216–275), who was brought up in Babylon as an Elchasaite, a Jewish-Christian sect which was, interestingly, also known as *katharoi*. After a series of revelations, Mani attempted to reform the Elchasaites, but was denounced and thrown out. Undeterred, he began a vigorous missionary campaign with three former Elchasaites (one of whom was his father) to proselytise what Mani called the Religion of Light. Mani claimed that he was of the same tradition as Zoroaster, the Buddha and Jesus, but that these earlier masters had not revealed the whole truth, the revelation of which was his mission and his alone. Mani's doctrine was formulated to appeal to as many people as possible; it was, in effect, a cut-and-paste religion – taking ideas from Zoroastrianism, Christianity and Buddhism – whose aim was to unite and save humanity in one overarching faith. There were two distinct classes of Manichaean, the Elect and the Listeners. The Elect were the faith's priesthood, and practised strict asceticism, abstaining from meat, wine, blasphemy and sex. The Listeners – the rank and file believers of Mani's church – were also expected to observe certain rules, including contributing to the upkeep of the elect, and, while they were allowed to own property and marry, they were forbidden to have children. While Mani's system is too complicated to go into here at length, it should be noted that Manichaeism is radically dualist, denying the validity of baptism, holding that Christ did not suffer on the cross, rejecting the body as irredeemable and maintaining that the evil principle is the equal of the good.

To the church, Manichaeism was the deadliest of heresies, even worse than Marcionism. It enjoyed widespread popularity, and St Augustine of Hippo was a Listener of the sect for nine years. When the preaching of St Ambrose and an epiphany in a garden in Milan turned Augustine towards Christianity in 386, he denounced Manichaeism in *De Manichaeis* and *De Heresibus*, which were to become the Church's standard reference books on all matters heretical, and were frequently used in order to identify suspected heretics when the Great Heresy began to emerge in the west from the end of the tenth century onwards. To Augustine, his former faith was a perversion of the truth of the Gospels, its missionaries and priests deceitful and cunning.

With Augustine its most vocal and authoritative opponent, Manichaeism began to go into decline. As early as 372, Manichaeans were forbidden from congregating, and the Roman emperor Theodosius the Great (379–95) – who made Christianity the state religion in 380 – passed legislation against them. The fifth and sixth centuries saw a concerted effort by Rome to wipe out Mani's followers, while similar measures were enacted in the Byzantine Empire. Early in his reign, the Byzantine emperor, Justinian the Great (527–65), introduced the death penalty for Manichaeans, the favoured method of despatching adherents of the Religion of Light being by burning. So effective was the persecution under Justinian that, by the

31

time of his death in 565, Manichaeism had been effectively wiped out altogether in the west. The Church was tightening its grip.[26]

Manichaeism might have been extinguished from Europe, but the name lived on as a byword for dualist, heretic or merely a political opponent. (Indeed, the word 'maniac' derives from a derogatory term for Manichaean.) Heresy moved east and Armenia, despite being the first Christian nation, was fast becoming a hotbed of heresy courtesy of refugees fleeing from persecution in the Byzantine Empire and elsewhere. Two new dualist heresies emerged to take the place of Manichaeism: Massalianism and Paulicianism. The Massalians, who were also known as the Enthusiasts (from the Greek *enthousiasmos*, which comes from the word *entheos*, 'having the God within') were originally from north-east Mesopotamia, where they are thought to have originated in the late fourth century. As early as 447, Massalianism was already perceived as the biggest heretical threat in Armenia, and the Armenian church introduced measures against its followers. Their main tenet of faith seems to have been the belief that inside every person dwells a demon, who must be banished through a life of prayer (the name 'massalian' means 'praying people') and asceticism. Once the demon had been banished, the possibility of further sinning was deemed impossible and the believer could return to secular life. As a consequence, the Massalians were frequently accused of immorality and licentiousness. Their missionaries frequently targeted monasteries; any house suspected of being infected with their heresy risked being burnt to the ground.

The Paulicians were first noted in sixth-century Armenia. Whether the Manichaeans influenced them is debatable, as the

Paulicians did not divide their number into Elect and Listeners, as the Manichaeans had done, and neither were they particularly ascetic. The exact date at which the Paulicians became dualists – they seem originally to have been Adoptionists, who believed that Christ was born human and did not become divine until his baptism – is likewise debatable, and it may not have happened until the ninth century.[27] In a further deviation from Manichaeism, the Paulicians were fighters to be reckoned with. As the Cathars were pacifists, the Paulicians' military prowess was something of an anomaly. Seven Paulician churches were founded in Armenia and Asia Minor, whose mother church at Corinth was supposedly founded by St Paul, after whom the sect was named.

The Bogomils

As the long night of the Dark Ages descended over Europe, the Church faced threats from two different sources: the rise of the new religion of Islam, which began to make rapid inroads into Christian kingdoms from the early eighth century, and the waves of nomadic invasions that began with the Huns in the fourth century. The Church's position was further weakened by its constant struggles with the eastern Orthodox church, a situation that worsened until the dramatic schism of 1054 rent the eastern and western churches permanently asunder. The Balkans, falling midway between Rome and Constantinople, became a theological battleground, serving as home to numerous heterodox sects as much as Armenia had done a century or two before.

The decisive development that paved the way for the Cathars' great predecessors, the Bogomils, was the establishment of the first Bulgarian empire (681–1018). Bulgaria immediately proved to be a thorn in Constantinople's side, and the fact that it was pagan only exacerbated matters. In order to create a bulwark against Bulgaria, colonists from the Byzantine empire's eastern edges were forcibly resettled in Thrace – an area roughly comprising north-eastern Greece, southern Bulgaria and European Turkey. Unfortunately, amongst those being repatriated were the Paulicians. Introducing heretics into an area that bordered on a pagan kingdom was simply asking for trouble, and trouble is precisely what Constantinople was to get.[28]

No one knows precisely where the Bogomils came from. They were first recorded during the reign of the Bulgarian tsar Peter (927–69), who was forced to write twice during the 940s to the patriarch of Constantinople, Theophylact Lecapenus, asking for help against the new heresy. Theophylact was known to be a man more at home in the stable than the cathedral, but he did have time enough to declare Bogomilism a mixture of Manichaeism and Paulicianism. A serious riding accident prevented him from giving Peter more help, and the new dualist faith continued to grow at an alarming rate, so much so that a Bulgarian priest known as Cosmas was forced to denounce the new sect in his *Sermon Against the Heretics*, which was written at the very end of Peter's reign (it was certainly completed by 972).

Cosmas writes that the sect was founded by a priest named Bogomil, but there is both controversy over what his name means and whether it was his real name at all. Some interpret Bogomil as meaning 'beloved of God', while others opt for 'worthy of God's mercy' and 'one who entreats God'. Cosmas describes the Bogomils as rejecting the Old Testament and Church sacraments; the only prayer they used was the Lord's Prayer. They did not venerate icons or relics, while the cross was denounced as the instrument of Christ's torture. The Church itself was seen as being in league with the devil, whom the Bogomils regarded as not only the creator of the visible world, but also as Christ's brother. Their priests were strict ascetics, and they abstained from meat, wine and marriage. The Bogomils were – at least initially – mitigated dualists, regarding the devil as a fallen angel who was inferior to God. They knew the scriptures inside out, but what puzzled Cosmas was the way in which they interpreted them. For instance, in the parable of the Prodigal Son (Luke 15.11–32), they saw the elder, stay-at-home, son as being Christ, while the younger, prodigal, son was Satan. The Bogomil take on the Crucifixion was Docetic.

The Bogomil Church was divided into two main classes, the Perfect and the Believers, similar to the Manichaean Elect and Listeners, although the Bogomils apparently did have a Listener class as well, who were below the Believers. According to the monk Euthymius of Constantinople, who was writing in about 1050, the Bogomil Listener became a Believer by way of a baptism that included placing the gospel on the initiate's head, while the actual baptism itself was done not by water, but by the laying-on of hands. As far as Euthymius was concerned, this erased the Christian baptism, and put the new Believer firmly under the sway of the Evil One.

The road from Believer to Perfect was a long and arduous one, with intensive teachings, ascetic practices and study, which took two years or more to complete. The ceremony in which a

Believer became a Perfect was similar to that which made a Listener a Believer, and was known as the *consolamentum* (the consoling), or *baptisma*. For Euthymius, it was 'whole heresy and madness' and 'unholy service to the devil and his mysteries',[29] yet the Bogomils regarded themselves as being the heirs to true, apostolic Christianity. Modelling themselves on Christ and the Apostles, Bogomil leaders had 12 disciples and lived lives of simplicity and poverty, in reaction to what they saw as the irredeemable corruption and false teachings of the Church.

What further worried Euthymius was that the Bogomils seemed to be a fully developed counter-church, one whose missionaries were active in spreading the word of the heretical faith. How, when and where the Bogomils organised is still a matter of debate, but it seems that, right from the time when they were noted during Tsar Peter's reign, they were already a distinct group, with their own teachings. Again, whether they were influenced by the Paulicians, Manichaeism or Zoroastrianism is a matter of conjecture. Amongst the Bogomils whose names have survived are Jeremiah (thought by some to be the pseudonym of Bogomil himself), who wrote the widely circulated tract *The Legend of the Cross*, and two extremely obscure individuals called Sydor Fryazin and Jacob Tsentsal, who brought heretical books with them into Bulgaria. Interestingly, both men were described as being Franks (the name 'Fryazin' means 'Frank'), which raises the possibility that there were heretical groups active in the west around the time that Bogomilism first became known. In Asia Minor, John Tzurillas and Raheas were active Bogomil proselytisers during the eleventh century who, like the Massalians before them, specialised in infiltrating monasteries.

Perhaps the most notable Bogomil after the movement's founder was the heresiarch Basil the Physician, who was active in the latter part of the eleventh century. It is said that his ministry lasted for 52 years before he was unmasked during the anti-heretical campaigns of the Byzantine emperor, Alexius Comnenus (1081–1118). Heresy was much on the emperor's mind by the late eleventh century: northern Thrace in particular had become an epicentre of Paulicianism, and Alexius resolved to bring its followers back into the fold of orthodoxy by whatever means necessary. This resulted in a number of armed confrontations with the Paulicians, whose reputation for being fierce warriors preceded them. Sometimes, though, the means by which the heretics were brought back to the fold took the form of protracted debates in which the emperor indulged his enthusiasm for religious disputation. Such a dispute duly occurred sometime around the year 1100, with Basil being invited to the palace to explain his faith to Alexius and his brother Isaac. Basil duly outlined the main tenets of Bogomilism, before Alexius drew aside a curtain to reveal a stenographer who had transcribed Basil's testimony verbatim. The heresiarch was placed under house arrest in order that Alexius could try to win him back to the Church, but Basil refused to recant. During their talks, the house was afflicted with Fortean phenomena: it was subject to a rain of stones and an earthquake. Alexius's daughter, the historian Anna, took this as a sign that the devil was angry that his secrets were being revealed and that his children – the Bogomils – were being persecuted. Still refusing to recant, Basil was burnt at the stake.

Despite Alexius's efforts, the Bogomils continued to preach and win new converts, and the persecution against them in

Byzantium would have almost certainly driven some of them west. In doing so, the Bogomils seemed to be fulfilling an old Persian prophecy, which stated that, on the 1,500[th] anniversary of Zoroaster's death – which was interpreted as being the year 928 – Zoroastrianism would be restored. While the matter of the Good Religion's influence on the Bogomils is conjectural, the two religions did share one thing in common: Dualism, and by 928, Bogomil and his followers were starting their mission. As the twelfth century dawned, the prophecy seemed to have been well and truly fulfilled.

2

The Foxes in the Vineyard of the Lord

The First Western Heretics

At the turn of the first millennium, a peasant called Leutard in the village of Vertus, near Châlons-sur-Marne in the north-east of France, had a dream. In it, a swarm of bees attacked his private parts, and then entered his body – presumably through his urethra. The dream, rather than making Leutard wake up half the village with his screaming, inspired him to go into his local church, break the cross above the altar and desecrate an image of Christ. But he didn't stop there: he sent his wife away and began to preach openly in the village, urging whoever would listen that they should withhold payment of tithes. The bishop of Châlons got wind of the peasant's activities, but Leutard threw himself down a well before he could be apprehended. Leutard seems to have belonged to a group, although it is not known for sure whether it was Bogomil in origin. (If it was, we can safely assume that the bees were a unique addition to the original Balkan teachings.) Heresy had, despite these somewhat unusual circumstances, arrived in the west.

Heresy was also a phantom presence at the other end of the social and religious spectrum around the time of Leutard's singular ministry. Gerbert d'Aurillac, the first Frenchman to become pope – he reigned as Sylvester II between 999 and 1003 – made an unusual disposition at Rheims in 991 on the occasion of his consecration as Archbishop. He stated his belief in both the Old and New Testaments, the legitimacy of marriage, eating meat and the existence of an evil spirit that was lesser than God, one that had chosen to be evil. Since the Bogomils, and later the Cathars, rejected all the things that Gerbert was professing faith in, it has been assumed that he was either denouncing a Bogomil sect in the locality, or had himself been suspected of heretical leanings and was making a show of his orthodoxy.[30]

An obscure French peasant and a pope were not the only forerunners of Catharism. Vilgard, a scholar from Ravenna, saw demons in the shape of Virgil, Horace and Juvenal, 'who encouraged his excessive pagan studies.'[31] Despite his being burnt at the stake, Vilgard's teachings spread in Italy, and are alleged to have reached Sardinia and Spain, where his followers were supposedly persecuted. In 1018 'Manichaeans', who rejected the cross and baptism, appeared in Aquitaine, and four years later further 'Manichaeans' were sighted in Orléans. The Orléans heretics were in fact ten canons of the Church of the Holy Cross, a number of clerics and a handful of nobles, including Queen Constance's confessor. They were also accused of worshipping the devil in the form of an Ethiopian (Ethiopia being a byword for blackness and, therefore, ultimate evil),[32] rejecting the sacraments of the Church, denying that Christ was born of a virgin and denying the reality of the Passion and Resurrection. Furthermore, they were accused of holding nocturnal orgies, carrying out child sacrifice and performing magical flight – all of which would later recur in the Witch

Craze of the late Middle Ages and the Renaissance. But in 1022, witches were a threat as yet unperceived by the Church, and the Orléans group was burnt as heretics.

Burning at the stake had been the punishment for Manichaeans and would become the favoured method for dispatching unrepentant heretics. However, as the Church had had little experience of heresy for centuries, official procedure was non-existent and punishment varied greatly from area to area. A group of heretics discovered at Montforte in north-western Italy in 1025 was burnt, but at Arras-Cambrai a group which was unearthed the same year was merely forced to recant and was then given a copy of their renunciation in the vernacular.

As the eleventh century progressed, there were further outbreaks of heresy: during the 1040s, it flared up again at Châlons-sur-Marne; Aquitaine, Périgord, Toulouse and Soissons were also affected. It is impossible to say for certain whether these were all Bogomil-influenced groups: they were usually described by the Church as 'Manichaean', which became a blanket term to denote heretics – all clergy knew the term from St Augustine – despite the fact that most or all of them weren't. (In fact, Manichaeism during this period was at its most active in China.) While the usual arsenal of accusations – orgies, child sacrifice, eating a diabolical *viaticum* made of the ashes of a dead child – were never far away, in many of these incidents, there were a number of similarities. The groups were frequently ascetic, sometimes in the extreme. Church sacraments and the Cross were despised, as were the clergy themselves, while meat, wine and physical union were abstained from. Most of these groups, however, did not survive the death, imprisonment or recanting of their leaders, and heresy, a sporadic affair in the eleventh century, seemed to die out altogether from about 1050 onwards.

Church Reforms

That heresy seems to have died down almost completely in the second half of the eleventh century is possibly related to the fact that the Church was starting a programme of reform that had been initiated by Pope Leo IX (1049–54). The greatest of the reforming pontiffs of this period – and indeed one of the most significant of all mediaeval popes – was Gregory VII (1073–85). His tenure as the Bishop of Rome was an eventful one, which saw Gregory at odds with the senior clergy over issues such as celibacy and simony for most of his reign. However, perhaps Gregory's most influential act was to announce that the Church was the only means by which one could come to God. Every other church and faith was anathema. The Church was supreme, according to Gregory, with the pope himself being naturally the highest possible human authority. Gregory, as Malcolm Lambert notes, 'awakened in the laity a new sense of responsibility for reform and a higher expectation of moral standards from their clergy. A genie was unleashed which could never again be put back into its bottle.'[33]

Gregory was not the only one pushing for reform. One of the leading figures in the reform movement, Humbert of Moyenmoutier, the cardinal who placed the order of excommunication on the patriarch of Constantinople in 1054, thereby creating the great schism between the Catholic and Orthodox churches, wrote an influential treatise entitled *Three*

Books Against the Simoniacs, which has, in its revolutionary fervour, been compared to the *Communist Manifesto*.[34] The moral life of the clergy became the rallying point for reformers, dissenters and disaffected churchgoers alike, and such was their stress on the moral stature of the clergy that the reformers resembled the Donatists, the fourth-century heretics who held that the masses of priests with moral shortcomings were deemed invalid.

In the early years of the twelfth century, this popular reforming zeal became even more strident, with charismatic wandering preachers whipping up parishes and often whole towns into an anticlerical frenzy. Tanchelm of Antwerp (d. c. 1115), who was active in the Netherlands, inspired such fanatical devotion that his followers were said to drink his bathwater, and he did not travel anywhere without an armed guard (a measure which proved ultimately futile, as Tanchelm was fatally stabbed by an enraged priest). A rogue Benedictine monk, Henry of Lausanne, caused complete havoc in Le Mans, and effectively kicked out the bishop. Peter of Bruys was even more radical. In an echo of Leutard, he incited people to break into churches and destroy the crucifixes. He held public burnings of crosses until, one Good Friday in the early 1130s, an enraged mob threw him onto one of his own bonfires. Arnold of Brescia was even more extreme than Peter. A former student of Peter Abelard, Arnold launched an attack on Rome in 1146 and declared it a republic. It was not until 1154 that the pope was able to return to the Vatican. Arnold was burnt at the stake and his ashes disposed of in the River Tiber to prevent his disciples from making off with relics.

By the time Arnold made his stand in Rome, however, the

most serious heretical threat faced by the Church up to that time appeared on the banks of another river far to the north: the Rhine.

The First Cathars

The Cathars first emerged into history in 1143. Eberwin, prior of a Premonstratensian house at Steinfeld near Cologne, wrote to the great Cistercian reformer St Bernard of Clairvaux that two heretical groups had been discovered, after they had apparently blown their cover by arguing amongst themselves over a point of doctrine. The Cathars were brought before the bishop of Cologne for a hearing. It was discovered that their church was organised into a three-tier system of Elect, Believers and Listeners, much the same as the Manichaeans of Augustine's era had been, and they did not baptise with water, but through the laying-on of hands. They condemned marriage, but Eberwin could not find out why: 'either because they dared not reveal it or, more probably, they did not know.'[35] More ominously, the archbishop learnt that the heresy 'had a very large number of adherents scattered throughout the world' and that it had 'lain concealed from the time of the martyrs even to their own day [1143].'[36] Most of the heretics were persuaded to recant, although two of their number, apparently a bishop and a deacon, remained unrepentant even after three days' debate with both clergy and laity. Before sentence could be pronounced, the mob seized the two heretics and threw them onto a fire.

Another chronicle, *The Annals of Braunweiler*, notes that in the same year as the troubles at Cologne, heretics were also discovered at Bonn. They too were dragged before the

Archbishop of Cologne, where most of the accused either came back into the arms of the Church or managed to escape. The three that did not were burnt on the orders of Otto, Count of Rheineck.[37]

What was different about this new heresy was that it was not merely anticlericalism of the sort propagated by Henry of Lausanne and all the motley assortment of libertarian preachers who had been such a colourful – if unpredictable – fixture of religious life during the twelfth century up to that point. These new heretics had organised properly; indeed, the two groups discovered at Cologne were not merely dissenters from Catholicism, they were members of an underground church that had had time to build itself up and put itself in direct opposition to Rome and all that it stood for. As Malcolm Lambert puts it, '[the Cathars] offered a direct, headlong challenge to the Catholic Church, which is dismissed outright as the Church of Satan.'[38]

Nothing like this had ever happened before, and suddenly the new heresy seemed to be everywhere. Its rise concerned no less a churchman than St Bernard himself, who, after receiving Eberwin's letter about the events in the Rhineland, composed two sermons denouncing the heretics. He interpreted the 'little foxes' from Song of Songs 2:15 – 'catch the foxes, the little foxes, before they ruin our vineyard in bloom'[39] – as heretics. Bernard's tracts are full of the standard nay-saying: he warns of the heretics' cunning and secrecy, and accuses them of sexual misconduct and aberration. As to what could be done about the situation, he sounds as if he is almost condemning the burghers of Cologne who cast their Cathars into the flames: 'Their zeal [in rooting out heresy] we approve, but we do not advise the imitation of their action, because faith is to be produced by persuasion, not imposed by force.' He goes on to add, however, that 'it would, without a doubt, be better that they should be coerced by the sword of him "who beareth not the sword in vain" than that they should be allowed to draw away many other persons into their error.'[40] In other words, he doesn't mind people being quietly heretical at home, but once they start to proselytise, then they are asking for trouble. As for punishment, the worst thing he advises is expulsion from the Church. In light of what was to happen in the Languedoc in the early years of the following century, Bernard's views are remarkably humane and tolerant. If the Church had listened to him – he was after all the most powerful figure in the Church of his time – history might have been different.

Bernard himself visited the Languedoc in 1145, suspicious that the Count of Toulouse, Alfonso-Jordan, was not doing enough to check the apparent growth of heresy in his lands. Whether Bernard's visit happened before or after he composed his brace of anti-heretical sermons, we don't know. What we do know, however, is that the man famed for his preaching skills met a decidedly mixed reaction. He got off to a good start in Albi. The papal legate there was not the most popular of people, and Bernard knew he had to make his words count. His sermon attacked Henry of Lausanne, who was then in the Albi area and was known to have supporters. It was a rousing performance. Concluding his sermon, Bernard asked all those in the congregation who accepted the Catholic Church to raise their right hand. Everyone put their hands up. It marked the end of Henry's support in the Languedoc.

If Henry's career was at an end, then events in the village of

Verfeil to the north-east of Toulouse made Bernard realise other forms of heresy were still very much alive and well. He preached in the church, but when he tried to deliver another sermon outside to those who could not get in, his words were drowned out by local knights clashing their armour. Bernard was laughed out of town. The incident could be ascribed to anticlericalism, which was rife in the south at the time, as much as to heresy, but to Bernard there was only one explanation. He returned fuming to his monastery in Champagne, declaring the whole of the Languedoc 'a land of many heresies' that needed 'a great deal of preaching'.[41]

The 'great deal of preaching' urged by Bernard was largely unforthcoming. Christendom had more pressing matters on its hands in the shape of the Second Crusade, with Bernard himself taking an active role in its early stages. However, once the Crusade was on its way to the east, the pope, Eugenius III, did try to do something about the growth of heresy by issuing a papal bull in 1148 forbidding anyone from helping heretics in Gascony, Provence and elsewhere. In 1157, the Archbishop of Rheims presided over a meeting of the provincial council, which condemned a group of heretics called *Piphles,* which rejected marriage. At the Council of Tours in 1163, Pope Alexander III presided over a gathering of cardinals and bishops which reiterated Eugenius's directives by passing legislation directed against 'Albigensians' – so-called because the Great Heresy was flourishing unchecked in the town of Albi – and those who helped them. The same year, Hildegard of Bingen had an apocalyptic vision in which she saw the emergence of the Cathars as evidence that the devil had been released from the bottomless pit. Only destruction could now come to mankind.

The year 1163 also saw the first detailed refutation of Catharism by a member of the Church. Eckbert, Abbot of Schönau, wrote a set of 13 sermons with the overall title of *Sermones contra Catharos* for Rainald of Dassel, who was the imperial chancellor and Archbishop of Cologne. Although the *Sermones* are peppered with large chunks of St Augustine's *De Manichaeis* to back up the argument, Eckbert had had personal experience of debating with Cathars in the 1150s, and it is this that makes us certain that the heretics he is describing are Cathars and not merely anticlerical trouble-makers in the mould of Henry of Lausanne and his ilk. After a short preamble, Eckbert begins to tackle the major tenets of Catharism, refuting each one as he goes along. He goes on to say that they hate the flesh, and avoid all contact with it, both in terms of procreation and dietary habit. Eckbert goes on to say that they are called Cathars, but are known under other names in other places: *Piphles* in Flanders, *Texerant* in France. No one knows the origin of the word or precise meaning of *Piphles*, while *Texerant* was derived from the term for weaving. Weaving was one of the professions forbidden to the clergy, being associated with heresy and magic, but the Cathars, while professing hatred for the world, realised the need to earn a living while in it and often worked as weavers.

While Eckbert's treatment of Catharism has thus far been reasonably reliable, it is when he tries to explain the origins of the word 'Cathar' that he starts to enter the realms of conjecture. He says that the first Cathars, whom, he believed, lived in antiquity, took their name from *katharos*, the Greek word for 'pure'. In linking the Cathars with the apostolic era, Eckbert is inadvertently supporting the Cathars' own claims that they were descended from the time of the apostles. And Cathars, it must be remembered, were legislated against at the Council of Nicea. So were the Cathars of the fourth century the same as the Cathars of the twelfth? Probably not. And the name is, again, probably not derived from *katharos*, but, as Alan of Lille (*c.*1128–1202) says, 'from the cat, because, it is said, they kiss the posterior of the cat, in whose form, as they say, Lucifer appears to them.'[42]

The Living Icons

The Cathars, or Good Christians as they called themselves, would certainly have been horrified to learn they were being referred to in derogatory terms that suggested they were participants in fictitious satanic ceremonies that were the product of rumour and the overactive imaginations of Catholic critics. Although the Church was keen to paint heretics of all denominations in the blackest possible colours, in doing so they frequently resorted to cliché and outright fabrication; much the same happened to the Jews, who were said to steal Christian children and sacrifice them in secret. In fact, the Cathars were far from satanic, and were often regarded as being better Christians than their Catholic counterparts, a fact which the Church was later forced to acknowledge.

If their virtue set them apart, then the Cathars' beliefs further removed them from the mainstream of Christian life. They inherited much from the Bogomils. Like them, the Cathar faith was dualist, holding that the material world is evil, the creation of the devil himself. The true god existed in a world of eternal light beyond the dark abyss of human existence. Both the Cathars and the Bogomils rejected the Church and all its sacraments completely, regarding it as the Church of Satan. The only sacrament they observed was the *consolamentum*, which served as baptism or, if administered on the deathbed, extreme unction. The only prayer both churches used was the Lord's Prayer, with the Cathars substituting 'supersubstantial bread' for 'daily bread'. Both Bogomils and Cathars alike rejected most of the Old Testament – and its belligerent deity – as satanic.[43] Both movements regarded the entity of the Church – Catholic in the west, Orthodox in the east – as the Church of Satan, and rejected it utterly. Church buildings – the churches, chapels and cathedrals themselves – were likewise seen as no more holy than any other building, and neither sect built any, preferring instead to meet in people's homes, or in barns or fields. Contemporaneous anti-dualist propaganda tells of a Bogomil monk who, feigning orthodoxy, built a church on the banks of the Bosphorous, but put a latrine in behind the altar, thereby desecrating it, while in Toulouse, a Cathar was said to have entered a local church and emptied his bowels on the altar, cleaning himself up with the altar cloth.[44] The Cross was seen as the instrument of Christ's torture, and Bogomils and Cathars alike refused to venerate it. They interpreted the Eucharist allegorically, and took the Docetic line on Christ's nature, his miracles, Passion and Resurrection. Cathars and Bogomils alike regarded marriage as fornication, and saw it as a means by which further souls could be entrapped in matter through the thoroughly distasteful business of childbirth. While there is little or no evidence about women in the Bogomil church, the Cathars regarded women as the equal of men, and Catharism offered women the chance to participate fully in the faith at all levels.

The structure of the Cathar church was again derived from the Bogomil model. Cathars were divided into three classes: Listeners, Believers and Perfect. The Listeners were people who chose not to commit to the faith wholeheartedly; they might hear the occasional sermon, but no more. At this stage, Listeners would hear sermons that were close in spirit to evangelical Christianity. If they chose to become a Believer, they would be asked to participate in a ceremony known as the *convenanza*, which formally bound them to the Cathar church. Believers formed the majority of the movement. They were ordinary men and women who had ordinary jobs and who lived in towns or villages. They were not cut off in monastic seclusion, did not have to abstain from meat, wine or sex, but were very much involved in the world of matter. They were taught to be in the world, but not of it, to follow the basic teachings of the Gospels, to love one another, to live a life of faith and to seek God. They were generally not exposed to dualist doctrine, which was nearly always reserved for the ears of the Perfect alone. The Perfect were the austere, top-level Cathars who were effectively the movement's priesthood. Both Cathars and Bogomils held the Perfect in the highest regard: they were seen as embodying the Holy Spirit, being the living church itself. They were seen as nothing less than living icons.[45]

The *Consolamentum*

Central to Catharism – like Bogomilism before it – was the baptismal rite known as the *consolamentum*. It was the means by which a Believer could become a Perfect, and thereby attain salvation. Without it, the Believer would be condemned to remain in the world of matter in their next incarnation. The *consolamentum* survives in two versions, one in Latin, dating from 1235–50, and one in Occitan, dating from the late 1200s, although both were probably based on one twelfth-century Latin original. The ceremony begins with a blessing:

ELDER:
Bless us; have mercy on us. Amen. Let it be done unto us according to Thy word. May the Father, the Son and the Holy Ghost forgive all your sins (repeated three times).

ALL PRESENT:
(The Lord's Prayer)
O our father which art in heaven, hallowed be thy name. Let thy kingdom come. Thy will be fulfilled, as well as in earth, as it is in heaven. Give us this day our supersubstantial bread. And forgive us our trespasses, even as we forgive our trespassers. And lead us not into temptation: but deliver us from evil. For thine is the kingdom and the power, and the glory for ever. Amen.

ELDER:
(John 1.1–17)
In the beginning was the word, and the word was with God: and the word was God. The same was in the beginning with God. All things were made by it, and without it, was made nothing, that was made. In it was life, and the life was the light of men, and the light shineth in the darkness, but the darkness comprehended it not.

There was a man sent from God, whose name was John. The

same came as a witness to bear witness of the light, that all men through him might believe. He was not the light: but to bear witness of the light. That was the true light, which lighteth all men that come into the world. He was in the world, and the world was made by him: and yet the world knew him not.

He came among his own and his own received him not. But as many as received him, to them he gave power to be the sons of God in that they believed on his name: which were born, not of blood nor of the will of the flesh, nor yet of the will of man: but of God.

And the word was made flesh and dwelt among us, and we saw the glory of it, as the glory of the only begotten son of the father, which word was full of grace and verity.

John bore witness of him and cried, saying: This was he of whom I spake, he that cometh after me, was before me, because he was ere than I. And of his fullness have all we received, even grace for grace. For the law was given by Moses, but grace and truth came by Jesus Christ. No man hath seen God at any time. The only begotten son, which is in the bosom of the father, he hath declared him.

There then followed a series of requests for forgiveness, similar to the beginning of the ritual (in the Occitan version only).

The most senior Cathar present then placed the Book – either the New Testament or St John's Gospel – on a table covered with a cloth. The elder then explains in detail to the Believer the import of what he or she is about to do, and takes the would-be Perfect through a line-by-line exegesis of the Lord's Prayer. When this is over, the ceremony continues:

ELDER:

Now you must understand if you would receive this prayer, that it is needful for you to repent of all your sins and to forgive all men, for in the Gospel Christ says, 'But and ye will not forgive men their trespasses, no more shall your father forgive your trespasses.' (Matthew 6.15)

Sometimes there was a break in the ceremony at this point, but it was not mandatory. What followed next was the actual *consolamentum* itself.

ELDER:

[Name of Believer], you wish to receive the spiritual baptism by which the Holy Spirit is given in the Church of God, together with the Holy Prayer and the imposition of hands by Good Men. This holy baptism, by which the Holy Spirit is given, the Church of God has preserved from the time of the apostles until this time and it has passed from Good Men to Good Men until the present moment, and it will continue to do so until the end of the world. [Name of Believer] keep the commandments of Christ to the utmost of your ability. Do not commit adultery, kill, lie, nor swear an oath nor steal. You should turn the other cheek in the face of those that persecute you. You must hate this world and its works and the things that are of this world.

BELIEVER:

I will.

The Believer gives the elder the *melioramentum*, or ritual greeting, by which Believers honoured the Perfect.

The elder then takes the Book from the table and places it on the Believer's head, and all the Perfect present place their right hand on the Believer.

The ceremony ends with further requests for forgiveness, and the ritual known as the Act of Peace, in which all present kiss each other on the cheek, and also kiss the Book. The Believer is consoled. He or she is now a Perfect.[46]

As a Perfect, they would now be expected to keep their vows for the rest of their lives. The slightest slip would necessitate reconsoling, and also invalidate the *consolamentums* of any Believers they may have made perfect. This was known euphemistically as 'making a bad end'. They were expected to pray fifteen times a day, and to fast on Mondays, Wednesdays and Fridays. Prayers were to be said on horseback, when crossing rivers and when entering the homes of Believers. When out travelling, if the Perfect – who usually travelled in pairs – came across goods belonging to someone, they were only to return them if they were sure the goods could be reunited with their rightful owner. If not, then the Perfect were instructed to leave them where they found them. If they happened upon a bird or animal caught in a trap, they were to release the bird or animal on condition that they were able to recompense the hunter with money or a gift. When visiting Believers, they were expected to bless them and their food if they were dining together, and would leave a gift for the Believers' trouble. Many Believers took the *consolamentum* when they were close to death, in which case, the cloth and Book would be laid out on the Believer's bed. If the Believer subsequently recovered, they were usually advised to seek reconsoling at a later date. Once a month, the Perfect in a given area would gather to meet their deacon and confess their sins, a ceremony known as the *apparellamentum*. Three times a year, the Perfect were expected to undertake 40-day fasts, mirroring Christ's experiences in the wilderness: from 13 November to Christmas Eve; from Quinquagesima Sunday (the Sunday before Ash Wednesday) to Easter; and from Pentecost to the feast of the apostles Peter and Paul (29 June). Aside from their rigorous observances, the Perfect were notable for their dress: they wore black, or sometimes dark blue or dark green, robes with a cord tied round the waist.

The Spread of Catharism

Once the Church had become aware of the Cathars, they also noted two things: that Catharism was already a fully fledged church that had suddenly emerged, as if from nowhere, and that the Cathars – along with fellow-travellers such as the Publicans and the Waldensians – seemed to be everywhere at once, undermining the foundations of Church and society. In Cologne, more Cathars were uncarthed the same year as Eckbert denounced the faith in his *Sermones*. Like their predecessors of 20 years earlier, they went to the stake. In England, a group of Publicans – who may have been Cathars under another name[47] – preached at Canterbury and Oxford, hoping to win new converts to the faith. They were denounced, branded, and thrown out into the winter snow, which no doubt did something to ease the pain of their burning skin. People were forbidden from helping them and were not allowed to give them shelter for the night. All of the Publicans were said to have died of exposure.

Another group of Cathars came to light in 1165 in Lombers, a town ten miles to the south of Albi. With their sensitivities heightened by the Council of Tours and Eckbert's pronouncements, the Church took the Cathars very seriously indeed. The heretics were arraigned before no fewer than six bishops, eight abbots, the local viscount and Constance, one of the king of France's sisters. The Cathars themselves knew that they had to be careful, as word would have no doubt reached them that their brethren in Germany had been burnt for their beliefs. Led by a Perfect called Olivier, the Cathars at Lombers engaged in debate with the clergy. They answered questions astutely, referring frequently to the New Testament. They came unstuck, however, over the issue of oath-taking: this was something they simply would not do under any circumstances. They claimed Biblical authority, citing Matthew 5.33–37: 'But I say unto you, swear not at all: neither by heaven, for it is God's seat: nor yet by the earth, for it is his footstool: neither by Jerusalem, for it is the city of that great king... your communication shall be yea, yea: nay, nay. For whatsoever is more than that, cometh of evil.' In mediaeval society, oaths were the glue that held things together: between lord and vassal, between Church and state. They were the middle ages' equivalent of modern legally binding contracts, and to refuse to swear an oath was an act of the greatest subversion. At this point, Olivier and his fellow Cathars went into a scathing tirade of abuse, denouncing the Church as hypocritical and accusing the assembled bishops of being little better than ravening wolves. However, unlike their unfortunate brethren in the Rhineland, the Lombers Cathars were allowed to remain at large. With anticlericalism running at an all-time high in the Languedoc, there were no doubt many people at Lombers that day who, while not necessarily supporting the Cathars in their beliefs, were unwilling to see them burnt. Such apparent toleration of heresy did not go unnoticed, and would not bode well for the future.

The Council of St Félix

The theological showdown at Lombers was nothing compared to what happened two years later[48] in the village of St Félix de Caraman in the Lauragais, south of Toulouse. The gathering of Cathars there in 1167 was 'the most imposing gathering ever recorded in the history of the Cathars.'[49] It was nothing less than an international symposium of Cathars from all over Europe, including – crucially – a delegation from eastern Europe. The purpose of the meeting seems initially to have been to reorganise the Cathar church, and to decide on important issues such as the creation of new bishoprics, the demarcation of diocesan boundaries and the appointment of new bishops.

Presiding over the council was the still enigmatic figure of Papa Nicetas. He had travelled to the Languedoc from Lombardy in the company of Italian Cathars (more of whom later), and was evidently treated with the utmost respect. The word *papa* is Latin for pope, but it is not certain whether he was one of the fabled heretical Balkan antipopes so feared by the Church. In all probability, he was a bishop of the Bogomil church in Constantinople, although it has been suggested[50] that he was merely a charismatic preacher exploiting western hunger for eastern wisdom. He may even have been both. We shall probably never know. What is known, however, is that Nicetas effected a profound shift in Languedocian Catharism, which would change the nature of the movement forever.

That a Bogomil bishop should be invited to chair an important Cathar gathering is the first real evidence we have of the kinship between the two heresies. While they shared numerous beliefs and practices, as we have already noted, strangely no evidence has come to light linking Bogomilism and Catharism prior to the meeting at St Félix. 'As far as extant records are concerned,' writes Malcolm Lambert, 'no Bogomil was ever caught preaching [in the west], leading a group of neophytes or disseminating literature.'[51] Quite how the Bogomils spread their dualist creed in the west therefore remains a mystery. Bernard Hamilton has suggested[52] that heretical Byzantine monks could have spread Bogomilism while on pilgrimages to shrines in the west, although where in the west they could have made their first landfall is open to conjecture. Palermo in Sicily seems to have had a Bogomil presence by about 1082, possibly due to Bogomils escaping Alexius's persecution back home. Bogomilism may have had another route into Europe via returning Crusaders, some of whom could have become infected with the heresy while campaigning in the east.[53] In short, we don't know for sure. The Bogomils remain amongst the most elusive of all mediaeval sects, and the lack of firm evidence about their activities in the west gives them the air of phantoms.

Catharism had almost certainly been developing quietly for some decades before the events of 1143 brought it to the notice of the authorities, and, despite its Bogomil ancestry, was 'never subservient to the East: as soon as we have records of its existence, it is unmistakably and thoroughly westernised and develops a life of its own.'[54] The Cathar faith as Nicetas encountered it in 1167 was rapidly expanding, and used the occasion of St Félix to put its house in order. The rambling diocese of Toulouse was split up: Toulouse, Carcassonne, and either Agen or Val d'Aran became bishoprics, and the border between Toulouse and Carcassonne was settled. One aspect of the Cathar church that remained intact, however, was the process by which bishops were elected. Each Cathar bishop would have two bishops-in-waiting beneath him, known as the *filius major* (elder son) and *filius minor* (younger son). When the bishop died, retired or resigned, the *filius major* automatically became the next bishop, and the *filius minor* became the *filius major*. A new younger son was then chosen. This helped maintain the unity of the Cathar church, and, in the case of the Languedocian church, helped to unify and strengthen it. Unlike the Catholic Church, there were no protracted rows about succession and election.

At some point in the proceedings at St Félix, however, Nicetas delivered a bombshell. He spoke of the unity of the eastern dualist churches, naming them as *Ecclesia Bulgariae* (situated probably in eastern Bulgaria or Macedonia), *Ecclesia Dalmatiae* (Dalmatia), *Ecclesia Drugunthia* (also known as *Ecclesia Dragometiae*, which was probably in Thrace or Macedonia), *Ecclesia Romanae* (Nicetas's own church in Constantinople), *Ecclesia Melenguiae* (location unknown, possibly somewhere in the Peloponnese) and *Ecclesia Sclavoniae* (also Dalmatia, possibly another name for *Ecclesia Dalmatiae*). While Nicetas claimed that these churches enjoyed cordial relations with one another, they did not in fact see eye to eye on matters of doctrine. The Cathars of the Languedoc were derived from the *ordo* – or rule – of *Ecclesia Bulgariae*, which meant that they were moderate dualists. Nicetas informed his captive audience, however, that the *ordo* of Bulgaria was invalid, as the person or persons from whom the Cathars of the Languedoc had first been consoled had made 'a bad end'. This was potentially disastrous news, as it meant that all the Perfect in St Félix that day were no longer Perfect. The issue was a crucial one, as the moral life of the clergy in the Catholic Church had been one of the main rallying points in calls for reform from eleventh- and twelfth-century critics, and the Cathars took some pride in the fact that the Perfect were wholly unlike the average Catholic priest in that they were actually holy; they practised what they preached, literally. To have the Perfect who had consoled you be exposed as sinful – even if it were only through a minor indiscretion – meant having to be reconsoled. Nicetas had a solution to the problem. His church in Constantinople lived by the *ordo* of *Ecclesia Drugunthia,* and he proposed that everyone accept the new *ordo*. There was one crucial difference between the churches of Bulgaria and Drugunthia: the latter were absolute dualists who were, in the eyes of Rome, even more dangerously heretical than the moderates. After some debate amongst themselves, the delegates at St Félix chose to accept the *ordo* of Drugunthia.

Catharism in Italy

As has been noted, Nicetas travelled to St Félix in the company of Italian Cathars. In Italy, as elsewhere in Europe, anticlericalism was rife. Arnold of Brescia's campaigns against the pope only ended with Arnold's execution in 1155, but stability did not return to the Italian peninsula. The papacy remained locked in conflict with the Holy Roman Emperor, the formidable Frederick Barbarossa, and a series of imperially sponsored antipopes. The situation was exacerbated by the influence of the Pataria, a group of pro-reform clergy which opposed the abuses of a mainly aristocratic clergy during the pontificate of Gregory VII. Like their brethren north of the Alps, the Pataria called for a morally pure clergy and remained deeply suspicious of conspicuous wealth and privilege amongst churchmen. The Pataria remained popular even after the movement's dissolution, and the time seemed ripe for someone to step into Arnold of Brescia's shoes.

According to Anselm of Alessandria, a thirteenth-century Inquisitor and chronicler, Catharism came to Italy from Northern France. Sometime in the 1160s, a 'certain notary' from that area encountered a gravedigger by the name of Mark in Concorezzo, to the north-east of Milan. Mark, evidently enthused by what the French notary had told him of the new faith, spread the word to his friends John Judeus, who was a weaver, and Joseph, who worked as a smith. Soon there was a small group of would-be Cathars in Milan, and they asked the notary from France for further instruction in the faith. They were told to go to Roccavione, a village on the road that led over the Alpes Maritimes to Nice, where a group of Cathars from northern France which followed the *ordo* of Bulgaria had established a small community. Mark received the *consolamentum* and returned to Concorezzo, where he founded a Cathar church and began to preach. Gathering followers, Mark spread the word in both the March of Treviso and Tuscany. It is probable that John Judeus and Joseph the smith also received the *consolamentum*, and began preaching careers. Further Cathar churches were established at Desenzano, in the March of Treviso (also known as Vicenza), Florence, Val del Spoleto and Bagnolo (sometimes known as the church of Mantua, which was nearby).

Nicetas's appearance, sometime prior to the gathering at St Félix, changed things in Italy. But unlike the situation in the Languedoc, where his mission had a unifying effect, in Italy he was to sow the seeds of discord. As he was to do at St Félix, Nicetas told Mark and his group that the *consolamentum* they had received was invalid, presumably as the Perfect who had administered it had also come to a bad end. Nicetas duly reconsoled Mark and his colleagues, and the group then accompanied Nicetas on his historic trip to the Languedoc. The situation, however, got dramatically worse after St Félix. Nicetas disappeared, presumably returning to Constantinople, never to be heard of again. In his place another eastern bishop appeared, Petracius from the church of Bulgaria. He informed Mark that Simon, the Drugunthian bishop who had consoled Nicetas, had been caught with a woman in addition to other, unspecified, immoralities. (Others believe that it was Nicetas himself who had made a bad end, thereby lending weight to the theory that he was something of a charlatan.) This left Mark and his group with no choice: they had to be reconsoled for the second time.

Mark set off, determined to seek a valid reconsoling, but was thrown into prison – presumably after receiving the *consolamentum* in the east, but before he could return to Concorezzo. John Judeus managed to speak with Mark in prison, and was reconsoled by him. However, John did not have the support of all the Italian Cathars, and some formed a breakaway group under Peter of Florence. At length, an attempt to broker peace between the two factions was made. Delegates from both sides went to the bishop of the northern French Cathars, from whom all the Italians had originated, to seek arbitration. The bishop declared that the matter should be settled by the drawing of lots, a precedent established in the Acts of the Apostles, where the disciples drew lots to elect Judas's successor. The winning candidate should go to the east, be reconsoled, then return to Italy and proceed to reunify the Cathar church. The plan was scuppered by Peter of Florence, who, in a fit of pique, declared that he would not submit to the drawing of lots. Peter then found himself out of the running, with John Judeus seemingly the winning candidate for the journey to the east. However, some of Peter's party were not happy with this arrangement, and protested. John Judeus, less of a primadonna than Peter, resigned, not wishing to cause further trouble.

In an attempt to sort out the mess, a council was convened at Mosio, which lay between Mantua and Cremona. The new plan was that each side would propose a candidate from their rivals. The chosen candidates were Garattus, from John Judeus's party, and John de Judice from Peter's. Again deferring to apostolic precedent, lots were drawn and Garattus was elected. Preparations were set in motion for his journey to the east: he started to choose travelling companions, and money was collected for the trip. Just as Garattus and his party were about to depart, however, two informers claimed that he had been with a woman. This proved to be the last straw and Italian Catharism splintered permanently. Desenzano remained faithful to the *ordo* of Drugunthia – and therefore Nicetas – and became a stronghold of absolute Dualism, while Concorezzo, Mark the gravedigger's church, reverted to the *ordo* of Bulgaria and moderate Dualism. The church in the Trevisan march took the middle line, and sent their candidate to *Ecclesia Sclavoniae*, which was impartial in the dispute between Bulgaria and Drugunthia. Unlike their counterparts in the Languedoc, the Italian churches would continue to bicker for the rest of the movement's existence.

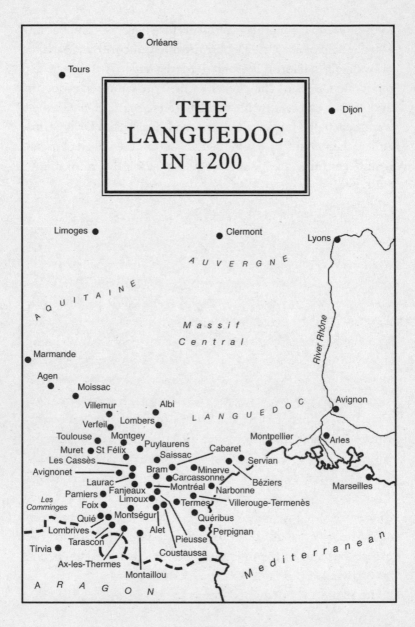

THE
LANGUEDOC
IN 1200

Orléans

Tours

Dijon

Limoges

Clermont

Lyons

AUVERGNE

AQUITAINE

Massif Central

River Rhône

Marmande

Agen

Moissac

Villemur

Albi

Avignon

Verfeil

Lombers

LANGUEDOC

Toulouse

Montgey

Montpellier

Arles

Muret

St Félix

Puylaurens

Servian

Les Cassès

Saissac

Cabaret

Avignonet

Bram

Minerve

Béziers

Laurac

Carcassonne

Montréal

Narbonne

Marseilles

Pamiers

Fanjeaux

Foix

Limoux

Termes

Villerouge-Termenès

Les Comminges

Quié

Montségur

Quéribus

Lombrives

Alet

Perpignan

Tarascon

Pieusse

Tîrvia

Ax-les-Thermes

Coustaussa

Montaillou

Mediterranean

ARAGON

3

The Albigensian Crusade

The Languedoc at the Turn
of the Thirteenth Century

The Languedoc in the year 1200 was a society in remarkable
flower. It was one of the most cosmopolitan and sophisticated
areas of Europe: trade flourished in the great towns of Toulouse
and Carcassonne, with Toulouse itself being only outclassed by
Rome and Venice in terms of size and cultural life. The arts were
enjoying a renascence, with the ideals of courtly love being
praised in the songs and poems of the Troubadours. Religious
tolerance was conspicuous, and Jews in particular enjoyed
freedoms that they were denied elsewhere. Woven into this rich
fabric was Catharism, which, by the turn of the thirteenth
century, was endemic throughout the Languedoc. Encouraged
by the momentous visit of Nicetas, the Perfect had been hard at
work for over a generation, spreading the dualist word
throughout the south, creating an heretical kingdom that
stretched from Provence to Aragon. That they had been so
successful is a tribute both to the temerity and faith of the
Perfect, but also to the unique way of life that the Languedoc
was enjoying at this high-water mark in its history.

The name Languedoc is a contraction of *langue d'oc*, the

'language of yes', a reference to the fact that in the region's native tongue, Occitan, yes is *oc*, not *oui*. The French language and those who spoke it were far to the north in the Île de France. Power in the Languedoc was shared between the counts of Toulouse, Foix and Comminges, and the viscounts of Béziers and Carcassonne. Although the Languedocian Cathars did not argue amongst themselves, the lords of Languedoc resembled the Italian Cathars: disputes were frequent, quarrels habitual, petty vendettas the norm.

The most powerful of them all was Raymond VI, count of Toulouse. His court was a kaleidoscopic mix of Catholic, Cathar and Jew, entertained by Troubadours and Jongleurs. His friends, as Stephen O'Shea notes, 'were not distinguished for their piety.'[55] Raymond had inherited his title in 1194 from his father, Raymond V. His parents seem to have been on opposite sides of the fence in matters of faith: Raymond's mother, Constance, had been present at Lombers in 1165 when the Cathars had faced down their Catholic opponents, while his father had invited a group of churchmen to investigate the heresy situation in his lands in 1177. They came, they saw, and promptly concluded that eradicating Catharism from the Languedoc was an impossible task, and went home as soon as possible. The one man whom they did manage to convict was sent to Jerusalem as penance. When he got back to Toulouse, far from having his tail between his legs, he was given a hero's welcome and was promptly given a well-paid job. This pretty much summed things up: as St Bernard had found to his cost, the Languedoc was indeed a 'land of many heresies' and respect for the Church was about as low as it could possibly be.

The Church during Raymond VI's early years as count of

Toulouse unfortunately deserved everything it got. The clergy were deeply unpopular: they were conspicuously indulgent, and there were churches where Mass had not been said in years. The locals used the phrase 'I'd rather be a priest' when asked to do something they would rather not. The bishop of Toulouse was a classic case in point: Raymond of Rabastens was a galloping financial liability. His main claim to fame seems to have been mortgaging church property in order to conduct a private war against his own vassals (done with the aid of mercenaries hired for the occasion). Raymond duly bankrupted the diocese, and was replaced with the more able Fulk of Marseilles, who had been a former Troubadour and was thought to be the only man who could handle the hornet's nest of the Languedoc. Such was the dire state of diocesan finances that when Fulk took over he did not dare send his mules to the well for water lest they be repossessed.

The moribund state of the Church was not helped by constant interferences from the nobility. The activities of the Trencavels — rivals to Raymond VI's family, the St Gilles — are a case in point. In 1178, they had the bishop of Albi arrested on trumped-up charges and thrown into jail, while the following year they forced an enormous sum of money out of the coffers of the monastery of St Pons-de-Thomières. In 1197, they contested the election of a new abbot in Alet, in the highlands of Languedoc. Their intermediary in the dispute, Bertrand de Saissac (several of whose family were Perfect), decided to show the Church who was boss: he dug up the body of the former abbot, propped him up in a chair and asked him who should be his successor. Bertrand got his way, a Trencavel puppet was installed and the late abbot was returned to his resting place.

In the midst of all this chaos, the Cathars were quietly, but firmly, spreading their faith. While the likes of Raymond VI and the Trencavels were either priest-baiting or conducting territorial wars against fellow nobles, the Good Christians were establishing themselves in home and hearth across the length and breadth of the Languedoc. Part of the reason for their success had to do with their respect for women, who enjoyed a higher status in the Languedoc than in most other parts of Europe. Primogeniture was non-existent, which resulted in estates being shared between sons and daughters. Although men were the largest landowners, women did at least stand a chance of being able to own property and thereby increase their status. Catharism helped women further: unlike the Catholic Church, the Cathars saw the sexes as equal, and there was nothing to stop any girl or woman becoming a Perfect. It is not surprising that women responded quickly to Catharism, given that the dualist faith actively encouraged women to participate, with the possibility of becoming Perfect and therefore semi-divine. The Catholic Church offered no such respect. In short, if you were a woman in the Languedoc of 1200, it made more sense to be a Cathar than a Catholic.

Cathar women therefore played a crucial role in the nurturing of the faith. While male Cathars travelled the countryside in pairs gaining new converts, the women established a network of Cathar houses; some of them, such as the houses at Laurac and Villemur, were exclusively for women. A number of the leading Cathar women of the early thirteenth century were also related to the nobility, either by blood or by marriage: Esclarmonde of Foix was the sister of Raymond Roger of Foix, one of the Languedoc's leading nobles, while

Blanche of Laurac, was married to Aimery, count of Laurac and Montréal.

Innocent III

The appointment of Fulk of Marseilles to the destitute bishopric of Toulouse was part of a wider plan of reform initiated by the new pope, Innocent III. Born Lotario dei Conti di Segni in 1160, Innocent studied theology in Paris and law in Bologna before taking the cloth. His rapid ascension through the Church paid its ultimate dividend when, on 22 February 1198, he was crowned pope. It was the end of a long and frequently disastrous century for the Church: 11 of the twelfth century's 16 popes had seen out their pontificates in places other than Rome, which was barred to them by the likes of Arnold of Brescia, rioters and foreign kings. The papacy was on shaky ground, too, with the Holy Roman Emperors. Frederick Barbarossa in particular had been a thorn in Rome's side for much of his reign, which had only come to an end when the emperor drowned crossing a river during the Third Crusade. Innocent was well aware of the troubles his predecessors had endured, and was determined to prevent history repeating itself.

The situation in the Languedoc was high on Innocent's list from the beginning. There had been periodic attempts to tackle heresy before his accession. Aside from the delegation which responded to Raymond V's invitation in 1177, the Third Lateran Council of 1179 had debated the issue of heresy, and decreed that force could be used to extirpate it. Two years later, Henri de Marcy besieged Lavaur, where two Cathars were known to be hiding. The town surrendered and handed over the Cathars, who were persuaded to return to the Church and became canons in Toulouse. Of greater significance was the papal bull *Ad abolendam*, issued by pope Lucius III in 1184. Although it focused on Italy as much as the Languedoc, it was the first direct attempt to deal directly with the problem of heresy. It denounced various sects – including the Cathars – and instructed clergy to make annual visits to parishes where heresy was suspected. However, Christendom had more pressing matters to deal with. The situation in the Latin east was deteriorating, and in 1187 it was overrun by Saladin's forces. Jerusalem fell on 2 October of that year, and suddenly heresy seemed to be of little consequence.

With the Languedoc's mixture of heretics, religious toleration, corrupt clergy and godless nobles, Innocent realised that action needed to be taken at once to prevent the already bad situation there from getting worse. In one letter, he described the clergy of Narbonne as 'blind men, dumb dogs who can no longer bark... men who will do anything for money... zealous in avarice, lovers of gifts, seekers of rewards.' There was no doubt in Innocent's mind as to who was the biggest offender: 'The chief cause of all these evils is the Archbishop of Narbonne, whose god is money, whose heart is in his treasury, who is concerned only with gold.'[56] Innocent tried to woo Raymond VI by lifting the excommunication the count had received in 1195 from Innocent's predecessor, Celestine III, for abusing the monastery of St Gilles. Raymond seemed little concerned, and so Innocent tried the more direct tack of writing him a number of letters, urging the count of Toulouse to do something about the Cathars. He did not mince his words. One letter rails at Raymond: 'So think, stupid man, think!'[57]

Innocent was not relying solely on Raymond, however, which was just as well, as Raymond was either unable or unwilling to persecute the Cathars. In April 1198, only two months after being made pope, Innocent commissioned the Cistercians to preach in the Languedoc with the specific aim of winning the heretics back into the arms of the Church. On 25 March 1199, he issued the bull *Vergentis in senium*, which equated heresy with the Roman crime of treason against the emperor, echoing the imperial statute *Lex quisquis* of 397. The punishment for heresy was to be the confiscation of property and the disinheritance of descendants. The civil right of election and of holding civil office was also forfeited. If the heretics were clergy, they were stripped of benefices; if they were lawyers, they were forbidden to exercise office as judges. Although it was initially intended to cover Italy, specifically Viterbo, whose Cathar population was militant and aggressive in a manner similar to the Paulicians, Innocent planned to extend *Vergentis* to other lands as soon as circumstance would allow. The following year, circumstance did just that, and Innocent suggested in no uncertain terms to the king of Hungary that he use *Vergentis* against heretics in Bosnia, while in the Languedoc, papal legates arrived to begin the work of smoking out heretics and confiscating their property.

Innocent potentially had another card up his sleeve. A dispute had arisen with the Hohenstaufen leader, Markward of Annweiler, who was acting as guardian to the child emperor, Frederick II. As a last resort, Innocent wrote to the people of Sicily (the Hohenstaufen court being in Palermo), urging insurrection against Markward. He drew parallels between Markward and Saladin, and offered Crusade indulgences to anyone who would take the sword against the German.

Although the plan came to nothing – Markward died in 1202 – it shows that, even at this early stage of his pontificate, Innocent was thinking along military lines when dealing with enemies. 1199 would indeed prove to be a turning point: a further Crusade against fellow Christians was theoretically possible. A precedent had been set.

An Enterprise of Peace and Faith

Innocent decided to replace his initial legates in the Languedoc – a certain John of St Paul and his companion – with three new recruits in 1203. All of the men were southerners: Arnold Amaury was no less than the Abbot of Cîteaux, while his two colleagues were both from the monastery of Fontfroide. Peter of Castelnau had been trained as a lawyer, and, like lawyers both before and after his time, had the habit of being violently disliked, so much so that he was subject to frequent death threats while on his tour of duty in the south. The third Cistercian, Brother Ralph, seems to have been the least troublesome of the three, and had at times to go into diplomatic overdrive to patch up the damage caused by Peter. They were universally loathed, and were to play a crucial role in the unfolding of events. Innocent referred to their undertaking as 'negotium pacis et fidei' – the enterprise of peace and faith.

The trio's first prong of attack was to try to force the local nobility to swear oaths of allegiance to the Church, in which they would also agree to anti-Cathar legislation. Failure to do so would result in instant excommunication. Toulouse, Montpellier, Arles and Carcassonne all agreed – at least in principle – with the measures the legates were proposing.

Raymond VI was not happy, however, as the anti-heretical statutes that the consuls of Toulouse had agreed to effectively diminished his rights as count. For the time being, he did what he had been doing all along when it came to persecuting the Cathars: nothing.

The trio's second prong of attack was to invite the Cathars to debate with them, in public, on matters of doctrine. Arnold, Peter and Ralph hoped they might be capable of rousing the people as St Bernard had done at Albi, rather than facing the humiliation the saint had endured at Verfeil. The first debate was held at Carcassonne in 1204, with Raymond VI's brother-in-law, King Peter II of Aragon, acting as the adjudicator as 13 Cathars faced 13 Catholics. The two sides defined their positions eloquently, but the debate ended inconclusively. The papal legates were unable to have the Cathars put in chains or on pyres, and left Carcassonne in a fume of frustration. It looked as though their efforts would echo St Bernard's defeat at Verfeil after all.

After Carcassonne, things only became more difficult for the legates. No one liked them being there: the Cathars naturally regarded them as the servants of Satan, but the clergy also were uncomfortable with the presence of the three Cistercians, no doubt fearful their cosy lifestyles and riches would disappear overnight. The nobility saw them as foreign meddlers, attempting to bring the ways of Rome to a land that had absolutely no need for them. Peter of Castelnau, already angry at the response he had so far encountered, tendered his resignation in 1205, begging to be allowed to go back to Fontfroide. Innocent refused his request. Although the pope did not know it at the time, he had just signed Peter's death warrant.

And so the trio plodded on, criss-crossing the Languedoc, haranguing nobles and disputing with the Cathars, but all to no avail – the heresy was too deeply entrenched. In Montpellier in the spring of 1206 the three Cistercians wearily concluded that they had failed. They were indeed in a land of many heresies, heresies that had defeated St Bernard and had defeated – and would probably outlive – the three legates. It was at this point that the luck of the campaign began to change. They were approached by two Spaniards, Diego de Azevedo, bishop of Osma, and his younger sub-prior, Dominic Guzman. Diego and Dominic told the Cistercians that they had seen the Perfect at first hand, and they had been struck by the Cathars' lives of the utmost simplicity, humility and poverty. The Perfect owned nothing except the clothes they stood up in and their holy books, a sharp contrast to the Cistercians, who travelled in pomp and circumstance with a retinue of lackeys and bodyguards. The Spaniards suggested that Arnold, Peter and Ralph take on the Cathars at their own game, citing the example of the Sending of the Seventy (Luke 10.1–12). The Cistercians were impressed, and agreed to the plan.

The summer of 1206 was a busy one, seeing the men adopting the apostolic model and preaching in poverty across the Languedoc. There were debates in Servian, Béziers, Carcassonne again, Pamiers, Fanjeaux, Montréal and Verfeil. As with the first debate at Carcassonne, these were lively and protracted affairs, sometimes lasting a week or more.[58] Without the usual Roman regalia to hamper them, they were getting results: 150 Cathar Believers were said to have been converted after the Montréal debate. But it was not enough. The enterprise of peace and faith had been in operation for three years, and the number of souls brought back to the Church was negligible for the amount of effort expended. By the spring of 1207, the preaching and debating seemed to have run its course, and Arnold Amaury left to chair a Cistercian conference. Peter of Castelnau was less easily dissuaded, and spent the rest of the year trying to get various Languedocian nobles to start rounding up the Cathars. Ralph followed in his wake, trying to keep Peter away from the crowds, almost all of whom detested him without reservation. In what debates remained, Fulk of Marseilles took his place. Dominic continued to preach, and even managed to found a convent for former Cathar women at Prouille.

Raymond VI again proved to be the stumbling block in the Church's path. Peter visited the count of Toulouse at a time when he was conducting one of his wars, this latest one being against his vassals in Provence. Peter wanted Raymond to turn his attention away from conducting private wars using mercenaries – who were a common feature of armed conflict in the Languedoc – and begin actively to persecute heretics. Raymond protested that he couldn't do without his mercenaries: they were a vital component of his power base. He refused to swear an oath of allegiance, and Peter excommunicated him on the spot. It was Raymond's second excommunication, but it would not be his last. Peter's final words on the subject echoed around the hall in which he and Raymond – and numerous other nobles – were gathered: 'He who dispossesses you will be accounted virtuous; he who strikes you dead will earn a blessing.'[59]

Raymond moved into diplomatic gear. He agreed to begin persecuting the Cathars and, by the summer, his excommunication had been lifted. By the autumn, having done nothing, he was excommunicated again. By now, patience was fraying on all sides. Innocent wanted action against the Cathars, while Raymond wanted the Catholic Church to stop meddling in his affairs. A new meeting was arranged at Raymond's castle at St Gilles in early 1208. Exchanges between Raymond and Peter were heated, with the count threatening physical violence against the papal legate. On Sunday, 13 January, negotiations broke down completely. Peter left for Rome at first light next morning. He was never to get there. While waiting for the ferry across the Rhône, a hooded rider galloped up to Peter and put a sword through him. The identity of the assassin remains unknown, but it mattered little: it was now war.

The Albigensian Crusade

When Innocent heard the news, he was said to have buried his face in his hands, before going off to St Peter's to pray.[60] Raymond was not forthcoming with an apology, and, although it could not be proved that he had ordered Peter's murder, his lack of apology was seen as an admission of guilt. It was a diplomatic blunder of monumental proportions. That Peter had so many enemies in the Languedoc that the list of potential suspects could have included most of the nobility and the clergy was irrelevant.[61] Innocent was convinced of Raymond's complicity in the killing, and, on 10 March, called for a Crusade. The use of force had been in the air ever since the trouble with Markward of Annweiler, and Innocent had been considering a campaign in the south since at least the previous November. The Crusade was to be preached by Arnold Amaury and Fulk of Marseilles, who spent the better part of 1208 rallying support from kings and nobles across Europe. Most were too busy fighting each other to go off and do the pope's bidding, but Arnold's and Fulk's persistence paid off and, by the middle of the following year, a ragtag army of nobles, knights and mercenaries were on their way. Innocent had given them the full Crusade indulgence: forgiveness of all sins, cancellation of debts and the promise of booty in the shape of land confiscated from the Cathars and their sympathisers. The Albigensian Crusade – like all Crusades before it – adopted the feudal custom that all who went on it only had to serve for 40 days before being released from their military obligations. The Languedoc also had the advantage of being easier to get to than the Middle East. Crusaders flooded down the Rhône valley in their droves.

Innocent had not given up entirely on diplomacy, but the deaths of Ralph of Fontfroide and Diego of Osma within 18 months of Peter's assassination had left the Church without two of its most valuable diplomatic assets in the south. Raymond had not given up on his own brand of diplomacy either. After failing to persuade Raymond Roger Trencavel, the 24-year-old viscount of Carcassonne, Béziers and Albi to join him in submitting to the Church – possibly as an attempt to keep the Crusaders off his lands – the count of Toulouse agreed to undergo a humiliating penitential scourging at the church of St Gilles. He was stripped naked and thrashed by a papal legate in front of two dozen bishops and a huge crowd of Toulousains, before being led into the church to swear allegiance to both the Church and the Crusade. He agreed to serve for the required 40-day period, but the demands forced on him did not stop there: he also had to renounce any claims he might have over religious institutions on his lands, and to apologise to all the clergy he had insulted, harassed and extorted money from. Seven of his castles had to be forfeited, as was the use of mercenaries, and all the Jews he employed had to be dismissed. When it came to the Cathars, he was to do as he was told: it was up to the Church, not the count of Toulouse, to decide who was a heretic and who wasn't. If Raymond stepped out of line, he was to be judged by papal legates. It was harsh treatment, and everyone knew it. The count of Toulouse had been made an example of. It was 18 June 1209, and apocalypse was only weeks away.

Raymond Roger Trencavel knew time was running out, but was confident that, as a Catholic, he would be able to parley with the Church. After all, most of Innocent's efforts had been directed against Raymond, the Cathars and their supporters who lived on his lands, and he must have thought that he was in a strong position. He was wrong. The Trencavels had a long record of antagonising the Church. In one of their boldest coups, Raymond Roger had kicked out the bishop of Carcassonne and installed a puppet. The new bishop's mother, sister and three of his brothers were all Perfect. Realising that Raymond VI had played a very canny hand by undergoing his scourging and submission, Raymond Roger also offered to submit to the Church, join the Crusade and take action against the Cathars. Arnold Amaury refused to allow this. The crusading army moved towards Béziers, while Raymond Roger retreated to Carcassonne.

Béziers – which had refused to hand over its Cathars to the Cistercians in 1205 – was annihilated on 22 July. Such was the scale of atrocity that even Crusade apologists such as Peter of Les Vaux-de-Cernay felt the need to distance themselves from it by blaming the bloodbath on the *ribauds*, the mercenaries. That such – even by mediaeval standards – appalling cruelty had been authorised by the papal legate, Arnold Amaury, was no doubt felt by some in the Church to have been justified. Arnold certainly thought so, and wrote to Innocent that 'the workings of divine vengeance have been wondrous.'[62] This view is echoed by the English writer, Gervase of Tilbury,[63] who described the situation in terms of a conversation between a priest and a ghost. The ghost told the priest that God had approved of the death of the Cathars, and that the citizens of Béziers had sinned because they had tolerated the presence of the Cathars in their town.[64]

The news of the atrocity at Béziers spread like wildfire. The Crusaders marched on Narbonne, which, fearing a similar fate, surrendered at the first sight of the Crusade. Carcassonne was next, and Raymond Roger Trencavel knew it. He implemented a scorched-earth policy around the city to make the land as inhospitable as possible for the Crusaders, who arrived on 1 August. The following day, the suburb of Bourg, which lay outside the city walls, fell. Further progress was halted by the arrival of King Peter II of Aragon, who asked to speak to Raymond Roger, who was his vassal. Peter informed Raymond Roger that he had brought the Crusade on himself by allowing Cathars – 'a few fools and their folly' as he described them[65] – to live unmolested in his city. Peter urged negotiations, as the size of the crusading army vastly outnumbered Raymond Roger's men. Talks began, and Arnold Amaury guaranteed Raymond Roger safe passage from the city once the surrender had been effected. The fate of the city's inhabitants would be left to the discretion of the Crusaders. Peter left in disgust at such terms and went back to Aragon. The siege dragged on. In losing Bourg and its wells, Carcassonne had lost its supplies of fresh water, and the city was soon suffering under a miasma of typhoid and dysentery. Raymond Roger was coaxed out of the city by a relative to negotiate. The precise details of the deal are not known, but Raymond Roger managed to save the lives of all the people of Carcassonne – including all the Cathars – on the condition that they leave the city. On 15 August, they did just that. They were not allowed to take with them anything more than the clothes they were wearing; many emerged from the gates barefoot. Arnold reneged on the promise he had made to Peter of Aragon, and had Raymond Roger clapped in chains in the dungeon of his own castle. He died there on 10 November, allegedly of dysentery. At the end of August, Raymond Roger's lands, and the leadership of the Crusade, passed to an obscure noble whose name was to become synonymous with ruthlessness and terror on a scale never before seen: Simon de Montfort.

Simon de Montfort

De Montfort was, until Carcassonne, only a minor feature of the Albigensian Crusade. He had distinguished himself during the attack on Carcassonne's other suburb, Castellar, and also during the Fourth Crusade, when he had refused to take part in the sack of the port of Zara on the Adriatic. This was not due to cowardice on Simon's part – he was a fearless warrior, almost suicidally so at times – but due to principle: the Crusade was meant to be attacking Muslims, not fellow Christians. He left the Crusade disillusioned. Simon's family were middling wealthy, with lands in the north, near Paris, and also possessed the earldom of Leicester, with which Simon's fourth son, another Simon, would become closely associated.

Arnold Amaury began to look for a successor to Raymond Roger after the fall of Carcassonne. He approached the nobles one by one, but all declined on political grounds, fearing a potentially jealous reaction from Philip Augustus, the French king. Simon, with his modest holdings in the north, was deemed a safer choice, especially as his military credentials and piety were beyond reproach. The Trencavel lands had a new viscount, and the Albigensian Crusade a new leader.

Simon's immediate problems were twofold: with the winter drawing on, most of the northern nobles returned home, and a number of the castles that had submitted to the Crusaders in the wake of Béziers had been retaken by southern forces. Indeed, resistance to the northerners was to be a near permanent feature of the Albigensian Crusade, and at Lombers there was even an attempt on Simon's life. No doubt such actions reinforced Simon's belief that he was fighting a just war; the towns and cities of the Languedoc were viewed – unlike Zara – not as Christian, but heretical, and the only way to bring them to submission was through merciless brutality.

The campaigning season of 1210 got off to just such a start. In early April, Simon had taken the small town of Bram after a siege lasting only three days. He ordered 100 of Bram's defenders on a forced march. Before setting off, the men were blinded, and had their noses and upper lips cut off. The man at the head of the procession was left with one eye intact, to guide his mutilated comrades to Cabaret, the nearest town 20 or so miles distant, which was known to be sheltering Cathars. It was the most hideous of warnings; Cabaret would fall to Simon within the year.

In June, the Crusaders besieged Minerve, a town perched on rocky cliffs 30 miles to the east of Cabaret. A huge trebuchet nicknamed The Bad Neighbour began bombarding the stone staircase that led to the town's wells, which lay at the foot of the cliffs. Once the wells were inaccessible, all the Crusaders had to do was wait; it would be Carcassonne all over again. Despite an unsuccessful attempt by the town's defenders to set The Bad Neighbour alight, the trebuchet continued to bombard the town into July. With their water supply cut off, Minerve's lord, William, had no other option than to surrender. He offered Simon all of his lands and castles on the condition that everyone within the walls of Minerve be spared. Simon agreed, and was just about to let the exhausted defenders of Minerve leave when the papal legate, Arnold Amaury, arrived.

Arnold, superior in authority to Simon, told William that everyone could go free on the condition that they swore allegiance to the Church. All the townspeople did so, but the Cathars were another matter. Swearing oaths was anathema to the Cathars, swearing one of allegiance to Rome unthinkable. Three Believers went back to Catholicism, but the rest remained unrepentant. On 22 July 1210, exactly a year to the day since the atrocities at Béziers, all 140 Cathar Perfect in Minerve were burnt in the valley below the town. It was the first mass burning of the Crusade. It would not be the last.

After Minerve, the remaining Trencavel *castra* – fortified towns – of Montréal, Termes and Puylaurens all fell to Simon's forces. It was while besieging Lavaur in the spring of 1211, that Simon's tactics reached new extremes of cruelty. No doubt enraged by the fact that reinforcements from Germany had been wiped out by Raymond Roger of Foix at Montgey near St Félix the day before they were expected to arrive at Lavaur, Simon's forces breached the walls of the town on 3 May. With flagrant disregard for the conventions of mediaeval warfare, all 80 knights defending Lavaur were hanged, as was its lord, Aimery of Montréal, who was suspected of being a Cathar Believer. His sister, Geralda, was famed for her generosity towards Cathars who had been displaced from towns that the Crusaders had taken. She was thrown down a well and stoned to death. All the town's Perfect – around 400 – were burnt at the stake. It was the largest mass execution of the Crusade. Later in the same month, between 50 and 100 Perfect were burnt outside the town of Les Cassès. If one were looking for proof that the world was, according to Cathar belief, evil, one would need to look no further than the events of May 1211.

Toulouse was next in Simon's sights, and the siege started the month after the bonfires at Lavaur. Within its walls, Raymond VI had not been having an easy time. He had been excommunicated yet again in September 1209 for failing to show enough commitment to the Crusade. The count then journeyed to Rome to bargain with Innocent, who allowed him to remain within the Christian fold, but only just. He then began a frantic diplomatic campaign, making good on all the promises that he had committed to during his scourging the previous June. Toulouse, meanwhile, was being terrorised by its bishop, Fulk of Marseilles, who had organised a vigilante group called the White Brotherhood, whose main occupation was nightly attacks on the homes of Cathars and Jews. In response, the Toulousains formed the Black Brotherhood, who clashed with the Whites on the city's streets on an almost daily basis. To cap it all, Raymond had been excommunicated for a fifth time at the Council of Montpellier in February 1211 after refusing to obey its directives, which would have restored him to the Church at the cost of abandoning all his possessions and giving up his titles. It was, therefore, a moment of respite when Simon called off the siege of Toulouse after only two weeks.

Peter II of Aragon was particularly sensitive to the threat posed to Toulouse and Raymond's lands. He attempted to negotiate with Innocent. He knew he was in a strong position: as one of the commanders of the crusading army which had achieved a decisive victory over Moorish forces on 16 July 1212 at the Battle of Las Navas de Tolosa in Andalusia, he was one of the heroes of Christendom. He argued that the Crusade had betrayed its original purpose – that of exterminating the Cathars – as it was now becoming evident that Simon de Montfort had killed as many Catholics as Cathars, if not more, and was also in the process of building up a nice little empire for himself. Peter proposed that he should oversee all of Raymond's possessions, which would then pass to the count's son, the future Raymond VII, when he came of age, leaving Peter to mop up the vestiges of Catharism that remained.

Innocent weighed up Peter's proposition, and was prepared to find in the Aragonese king's favour. On 17 January 1213, Innocent stunned Church forces in the Languedoc by announcing the end of the Albigensian Crusade, and instructed Simon de Montfort to return lands to the counts of Foix, Comminges and Béarn. Arnold Amaury protested loudly, arguing that the Crusade was still valid, as the Cathars remained very much at large. To make the situation even more tense, the remaining southern nobles – the counts of Toulouse, Foix and Comminges among them – agreed to Peter's plan to let him rule over all of the Languedoc, at least as long as the Albigensian Crusade was in operation against them. On 21 May, Innocent was finally swayed by Arnold Amaury, and reinstated the Crusade.

Simon de Montfort swung back into action, but, on 12 September, found himself confronted by a huge army of southerners led by Peter outside the town of Muret. Although greatly outnumbered, the Crusaders routed the southern and Aragonese forces. Not only that, Peter himself was killed. It was a disaster for the south, with at least 7,000 men being killed. It was de Montfort's greatest victory. He was now effectively the lord of all Languedoc.

The Fourth Lateran Council

November 1215 saw the biggest gathering of churchmen for centuries when the Fourth Lateran Council convened. Of its predecessors – the councils of 1123, 1139 and 1179 – only the latter had had any business with heresy, when it had been deemed acceptable to use force against heretics. By the time of the Fourth, that force had been a reality for six bloody and long years. Remarkably, the Fourth Lateran Council saw all of the major figures of the Albigensian Crusade in Rome, with the exception of Simon de Montfort and the Perfect. Even that veteran of excommunication, Raymond VI, was in town, as was the fearsome Raymond Roger of Foix. The southerners clearly had business with Innocent, and meant to be heard.

After a month of dealing with other issues – the preparations for the Fifth Crusade, the forcing of all Jews and Muslims to wear a yellow mark on their clothes to distinguish them from Christians – Innocent finally had time to address the situation in the Languedoc, which was, as ever, grave. Things got off to a bad start with Fulk of Marseilles, bishop of Toulouse, lambasting Raymond Roger of Foix for tolerating Cathars on his lands, and for his role in the massacre of Crusaders at Montgey. Raymond Roger retaliated, hurling abuse at Fulk and saying that he was only sorry he hadn't killed more Crusaders. It was all too much for Innocent, who had to go out into the gardens of the Lateran Palace to get away from the poisonous atmosphere inside and try to regain a clear head. When he came back in, he had decided to allow Simon de Montfort to retain all his lands in the Languedoc. Raymond VI's son, Raymond the Younger, would become heir to various smaller possessions, but Simon would now be officially the count of Toulouse. It seemed to be the final nail in the Languedoc's coffin.

The Siege of Toulouse

When Toulouse heard the news, there was uproar; the Toulousains were determined to keep de Montfort out of the city. He was, after all, universally hated. Resistance was compounded by the unexpected military victory of the Younger Raymond, who took the Crusader-held town of Beaucaire. Then Innocent died unexpectedly on 16 July 1216. It seemed as though things might be turning in the favour of the south.

Simon de Montfort's reaction was to hit Toulouse, and hit it hard. He was aided by that most charming of men, Fulk of Toulouse, who persuaded the city's dignitaries to discuss terms outside the city walls. Either Fulk was remarkably convincing, or the city fathers remarkably forgetful of what had happened to Raymond Roger Trencavel at Carcassonne, but they took the bait. They left the safety of the city, and were put in chains as soon as they reached Simon's camp. With no one left to coordinate its defences, Toulouse fell almost immediately to the Crusaders, who then spent a month sacking the city. To cap it all, Simon imposed exorbitant taxes on the beleaguered Toulousains.

At the moment of what was potentially his finest hour, Simon made a fatal mistake. Despite the fact that Arnold Amaury had recently excommunicated him for his bullying tactics in Narbonne, Simon blithely disregarded the excommunication and left Toulouse to harass the nobles of Provence, leaving a garrison to hold the city. The Toulousains immediately began to build up weapons secretly and devised plans to revolt against this most hated of men. On 13 September 1217, Raymond VI re-entered the city under the cover of dawn mist; the populace was ecstatic. Despite the fact that Raymond was an almost notoriously bad military commander – at the battle of Muret he had famously done nothing – the Toulousains felt that salvation was at hand. Raymond immediately ordered the rebuilding of the city's defences. Simon's garrison was terminated with extreme prejudice.

When he heard the news, Simon rushed back to Toulouse, intent on atrocity. Much to his surprise, he was thwarted time and time again. Despite the arrival of reinforcements from the north, Simon's forces could not breach the city walls. The stalemate lasted nine months, until June 1218, when the Crusaders decided, somewhat belatedly, to employ siege engines against the walls of Toulouse. On 25 June, during a defence of his siege engineers, Simon de Montfort's head was destroyed by a stone launched from a catapult on the walls of Toulouse. According to tradition, the catapult was operated by women and girls. The most hated man in the Languedoc was dead; no revenge was ever sweeter.

De Montfort's Impact on Catharism

With de Montfort dead, a chapter had closed in the Albigensian Crusade, yet it remains debatable what he had actually achieved. As Malcolm Barber notes: 'The relationship between Montfort's unceasing military activity and the actual extirpation of the Cathars is much more complex than the pope's rhetoric [of his call for a Crusade in 1208] suggests.'[66] Out of the 37 places de Montfort is known to have besieged, contemporary chroniclers record only three where Perfect were actually known to be (Minerve, Lavaur and Les Cassès). Although Cathars are not actually recorded as being anywhere else during the de Montfort years, 'it is probable that the Crusaders took it for granted that the defenders of places which resisted them must by definition at least be sympathetic to the heretics and their teaching.'[67] Furthermore, there were no fewer than 86 places on the eve of the Crusade where Cathars were known to have been living, of which de Montfort held 23 at one time or another between 1209 and 1218. This leaves 63 places that de Montfort did not attempt to take. It is possible that de Montfort was unaware of the presence of Cathars in some of these places, or besieging them may have been beyond his resources. Despite a crusading tax levied by Innocent, the Albigensian Crusade was not properly financed, and de Montfort had to rely on the support of private bankers and on obtaining booty to keep the Crusade afloat. The accusations that de Montfort, despite his piety, had a keen eye for booty and a desire for personal power are reinforced by the fact that he also managed to gain control of another 63 places that had no reputation for heresy whatsoever.

Most of Simon's campaigns concentrated on Trencavel lands or around Toulouse, and the odds of any given town being attacked were between three or four to one against. The Perfect therefore had plenty of places to hide, and hide they seem to have done, as there were no mass burnings of Cathars after Lavaur and Les Cassès. De Montfort was partially successful at breaking up the infrastructure on which the Cathars depended: there were no Cathar bishops of Albi, Carcassonne and Agen during his tenure, and only one deacon (in Carcassonne).[68] Cathar bishops seemed to have held office in Toulouse throughout Simon's years,[69] but they only survived by hiding at the Cathar stronghold of Montségur in the Pyrenees.

One partially successful policy had been the encouragement of crusading settlers in the south. The property of Cathars and their supporters, once abandoned, proved to be virtually impossible to get back, as they had been bequeathed to Crusaders such as Alan of Roucy, who took over Termes, Montréal and Bram, and Bouchard of Marly, who got Saissac and Cabaret.[70] Once installed, they were encouraged to marry local women, and thereby eliminate heresy through marriage. (Landed southern widows and heiresses required a licence to marry; Crusaders did not.) However, few of the settlers founded long-term dynasties in the south: they were either killed during subsequent southern uprisings, or went back north while they still had the opportunity to do so.

During the de Montfort years, diplomacy and preaching were still being used as weapons against the Cathars: Innocent never tired of trying to check the violence, and was constantly in talks with various ambassadors, legates and lobbyists. That he had to censure Simon in January 1213 shows how much he had come to distrust the military solution, and de Montfort's execution of it. It was not his military genius that was in question, but the sheer number of extracurricular sieges that he was undertaking, all in the name of increasing his own power base (indeed, after the Fourth Lateran Council, Simon held more land than the king of France, Philip Augustus).

However, the nine years of violence, brutality and terror did have a profound impact on Catharism. Before 1209, the Cathars had been able to pursue their faith quite openly. After that date, they became cautious and secretive, knowing they were hunted and might meet the same fate as the Perfect of Minerve, Lavaur and Les Cassès. De Montfort's other main achievement was to leave a legacy of hatred. The anonymous second author of the *Song of the Cathar Wars* spoke for many in the Languedoc when he wrote:

> The epitaph says, for those who can read it, that he is a saint and martyr who shall breathe again and shall in wondrous joy inherit and flourish, shall wear a crown and be seated in the kingdom. And I have heard it said that this must be so – if by killing men and shedding blood, by damning souls and

causing deaths, by trusting evil counsels, by setting fires, destroying men... seizing lands and encouraging pride, by kindling evil and quenching good, by killing women and slaughtering children, a man can in this world win Jesus Christ, certainly Count Simon wears a crown and shines in heaven above.[71]

The Changing of the Guard

Simon de Montfort's death heralded not only the end of one of the darkest eras in the west since the Viking raids, but also a period of change that saw the old figures die off: Dominic Guzman died in 1221 (in 1234 he would be canonised as St Dominic); Raymond VI died in 1222; King Philip Augustus of France died in 1223, the same year as Raymond Roger of Foix, who remained unrepentant and went to his grave wishing he'd killed more Crusaders; Arnold Amaury died in 1225. In their place rose sons and heirs such as Raymond the Younger, who would become Raymond VII upon his father's death, and Roger Bernard, son of Raymond Roger of Foix. Both men were able warriors, and played key roles in repelling the siege of Toulouse in 1218 and in subsequent southern resistance.

Simon de Montfort's son, Amaury, however, was not a chip off the old block when it came to military matters. After his father's death, he faced six years of constant conflict with Raymond the Younger and Roger Bernard. The de Montfort lands began to shrink on an annual basis. Amaury tried in 1221 to found a military religious order dedicated to fighting heresy modelled on the Templars,[72] but without success. His incompetence was to undo virtually everything his father had built up.

Innocent had long wanted the French crown to intervene in the south, but it was not until 1215 that Philip Augustus's son, Louis, finally launched an expedition of his own. Nothing much came of it. In 1219, he tried again, this time getting as far as committing wholesale slaughter at the small market town of Marmande, where all 7,000 inhabitants were killed, before attempting to take Toulouse. He wasn't able to, and went back to Paris.

The Albigensian Crusade further suffered under Innocent's successor, Honorius III (1216–27), who had another Crusade to deal with, the official Fifth, which began in the first year of his pontificate. While he saw the need to continue the fight against heresy, he did not put all his faith in crusading. He gave his blessing to Dominic Guzman's Order of Preachers (better known as the Dominicans) and the Franciscans; both orders were to expand exponentially in the following years, with both Dominic and Francis being canonised between 1228 and 1234.

The Perfect began to re-emerge during this period. Those who had survived Simon de Montfort had done so by hiding in caves, or in the Pyrenean fortresses of Montségur and Quéribus. In 1223, the Cathar bishop of Carcassonne, Peter Isarn, had copies made of the records of the meeting at St Félix so that he could determine and re-establish his diocesan boundaries after the havoc wrought by the Albigensian Crusade. In 1226, there was another major Cathar gathering at Pieusse. It was not as epochal as St Félix, but the fact that it happened at all showed that the Cathar church was far from beaten, and was confident enough to resume as normal a life as was possible: the council even established a new bishopric at Razès. But peace was not to last.

It was Amaury de Montfort who inadvertently brought more grief on the Good Christians. After several years of losing ground to both Raymond VII and Roger Bernard of Foix, Amaury and Raymond agreed a truce in the summer of 1223. In January 1224, Raymond took control of Toulouse, and the following month Amaury admitted that he was beaten. He ceded all his claims to the possessions in the Languedoc to King Louis XIII. The southern nobles now had one overpowering enemy: the French crown.

The Peace of Paris

King Louis was not the only person who wanted to settle matters in the south once and for all. The new papal legate to France and the Languedoc, Romano di San Angelo, was a ruthless and duplicitous man; perfect Vatican material and perfect for harassing the beleaguered nobility of the south, Raymond VII in particular. Raymond was operating under the supervision of the aged Arnold Amaury, who, since excommunicating Simon de Montfort, had – in the greatest irony of the whole saga – become sympathetic to the southern cause. Raymond and Arnold proposed a series of reparation payments to the de Montforts, in addition to Raymond swearing allegiance to the French crown and promising to drive the Cathars out of his lands. Romano, however, wanted the reinstatement of the Crusade, and made sure that Raymond's and Arnold's peace plan never got off the drawing board by excommunicating Raymond in early 1226.

Louis, for his part, was also keen on crusade rather than diplomacy, after getting the taste for mass murder at Marmande.

He was also aware that he could use the Church to bankroll the whole enterprise; it was the start of an era in which French kings would simply appropriate Church wealth for their own ends, and it ultimately led to the waning of Church influence in France. He and Romano haggled and argued over funding, until Romano managed to extract money from wealthy sees such as Chartres, Rheims, Rouen and Amiens.

In the summer of 1226, the Crusaders besieged Avignon. It was an uncomfortable stand-off lasting three months, during which Louis and his army succumbed to serious bouts of dysentery in the August heat. By the time the city finally surrendered, 3,000 Crusaders had died of the disease. But word spread: the great city of Avignon had capitulated. Even had they been able, the Crusaders would not have had to do much fighting; the size of their army was such that southern nobles were offering their submission on first sight of it, or even hearing that it was nearby. In the light of potential instant annihilation, former Cathar sympathisers such as Bernard Otto of Niort, the nephew of Aimery of Montréal and Geralda of Lavaur, suddenly became staunch supporters of the Crusade. The only real military challenges the Crusade faced were guerrilla attacks from the forces of Raymond VII and Roger Bernard of Foix, which proved a nuisance more than a real danger. Dysentery, however, would do more damage than the forces of Toulouse and Foix: Louis himself was now seriously ill, and died on 8 November in Montpensier.

Louis's son, the future Louis IX, was only 12 at the time of his father's death, and his mother, Blanche of Castile, became Regent. She was determined that her husband's death would not be in vain, and pressed on with the campaign to subdue the southern nobles and eradicate Catharism. With Cardinal Romano as her principal adviser – they were even reputed to be lovers – she ordered her armies to remain in the south and to finish what her late husband had started.

The late 1220s saw not so much a Crusade as a series of intermittent battles between Crusaders and southern nobility. It could have carried on indefinitely, were it not for the fact that, in 1228, the Crusaders began to employ an extreme form of scorched-earth policy. This was much more thorough than the one Raymond Roger Trencavel had ordered at Carcassonne in 1209; it was nothing less than the complete destruction of the countryside around Toulouse. Crops were burnt, orchards felled, sources of water contaminated. The skies were black for a whole year with smoke. By the beginning of 1229, with his lands an endless blasted heath that would take years to recover, Raymond had no choice: he had to sue for peace.

On 12 April 1229, history repeated itself. Raymond VII, like his father before him, was publicly flogged. It was to be known as the Peace of Paris, and the combined strength of Church and king had the count of Toulouse in a vice. Raymond's lands were seized by the French crown, leaving him with little more than the city of Toulouse and a few minor towns, which he was generously allowed to keep for the rest of his life, after which they would be incorporated into the growing kingdom of France. He was also forced to marry off his only child, a nine-year-old daughter, to one of the young Louis's siblings. In addition, Raymond was instructed to found – and fund – a new university in Toulouse, at which Church-approved doctors of theology would instruct new clerics in the ways of righteousness. It was the end of the Albigensian Crusade. Life would slowly return to normal in the Languedoc after 20 years of war, but St Bernard's original exhortation to catch the 'little foxes' before they 'ruined the vineyard' was now profoundly ironic: the vineyard of the Languedoc was indeed ruined, but it had not been the work of the little foxes. Although they did not know it at the time, the war-weary people of the Languedoc – both Cathar and Catholic – had little time to adjust to peace before they had to face a new terror: the Inquisition.

4

The Inquisition

While French troops reduced the Languedoc to the sort of
barren wasteland we might more readily associate with
Arthurian myth or the nightmares of Bosch and Bruegel, a
nightmare of another sort was being planned in the Lateran
Palace. Pope Honorius had died in 1227, and was succeeded by
Gregory IX, who was as much an activist pope as his great
forebears Gregory VII and Innocent III had been. Gregory –
born Ugolino dei Conti di Segni – was one of Innocent's
nephews, and was as legally minded as his uncle had been.
Gregory realised that if the Cathars were to be effectively
destroyed, then the Church needed the tools to pursue
individuals as much as, and perhaps even more than, the ability
to intervene militarily, as it was apparent that the dualists were
still active in the Languedoc and in other parts of Europe; the
discovery of Cathars in Rome in 1231 can only have hardened
Gregory's resolve.

The Inquisition was based on procedures drawn up under
Innocent to tackle wayward priests which gave Inquisitors –
usually Dominican friars – the powers of arrest and trial. What
started as a method for keeping the clergy in line was to become
'one of the most effective means of thought control that Europe
has ever known.'[73]

The First Inquisitors

The Rhineland, the haunt of the earliest known Cathars in 1143, was to receive the attentions of the first Inquisitor, Conrad of Marburg. Conrad was an extreme ascetic who brought a campaign of terror to the Rhineland with his two henchmen, Conrad Tors, a Dominican, and a one-eyed, one-handed layman called John. Almost everywhere they went, they found heretics of all denominations. Due to a combination of his own blinkered zealotry, and ignorance of what actually constituted Cathar belief, Conrad thought he had unearthed a heresy that he dubbed 'Luciferanism'. No doubt he remembered – or had it pointed out to him – that 'Cathar' meant someone who indulged in satanic rites which included obscene kisses on the rear ends of cats. On top of this fiction, Conrad constructed an elaborate demonology that possibly also contained elements of undigested Cathar doctrine, such as the belief that the devil had created the world. The heretics were thought to worship the devil and engage in sexual orgies. Such beliefs were not new: exactly the same accusations (minus the cats) had been levelled at the Orléans heretics in 1022. Conrad relayed his findings to Gregory, who promptly issued the bull *Vox in Rama* in June 1233 denouncing the Luciferans.

Conrad's procedure, if it can be called that, was swift and brutal. If the unfortunates whom the trio apprehended were adjudged guilty, they were burnt the same day without any further enquiries taking place. Hundreds, perhaps thousands, of innocent people – most of them simple, unlettered churchgoers – met their deaths. In amongst them were a small percentage of Cathars. The level of hatred Conrad generated was astonishing. He achieved a notoriety of de Montfortesque proportions within months. He went a step too far, however, when he accused Count Henry II of Seyn of heresy. Count Henry demanded the right to a fair trial, and Conrad's case against the count collapsed when it became apparent that the witnesses Conrad had called were amongst Henry's enemies, and the Archbishops of Trier and Mainz wrote to Gregory to complain about Conrad's behaviour. Conrad reacted by promptly calling for a Crusade against Henry and his supporters. On 30 July 1233, while Conrad was organising his Crusade, a local Franciscan decided to take matters into his own hands. He caught up with the Inquisitor as he was on his way back to Marburg from Mainz, and stabbed him to death.

Northern France and Flanders were subject to the attentions of Robert the Bulgarian, whose name suggests he was a Cathar who had renounced his former faith. Like Conrad, he was a fanatic of the most zealous kind, whose methods were 'ferocious and arbitrary'.[74] Chronicles report that Robert could detect heretics by foibles of speech and gesture; another spoke of a document, which, when placed on a suspect's head, made them say whatever Robert wanted.[75] Robert's crowning achievement was his participation in the burning of 180 heretics at Mont Aimé in Champagne in the spring of 1239. The area had been known for Catharism since the twelfth century, and the mass incineration was no doubt intended to spread further terror, and also to show bishops from around a dozen local sees what had happened to the heretics who had been uncovered in their areas. Robert was still conducting his idiosyncratic campaign against the devil and all his works as late as 1244, but was eventually disgraced and imprisoned for his excesses.

The Inquisition in the Languedoc

Gregory seems to have taken the complaints of the Archbishops of Trier and Mainz about Conrad seriously. While he castigated them for failing to keep the Inquisitor in check, he realised that if the Inquisition was to do its job properly, it needed to be much more methodical and thorough-going in its approach. With that in mind, Inquisitors were appointed in Toulouse, Albi and Carcassonne in the spring of 1233. It was with their arrival in the south that the Inquisition proper came into existence, and was to remain a grim fixture of life in the Languedoc for the next hundred years.

When the Inquisition came to a town or a village, the first thing its agents would do was to talk to the clergy, in order to brief them on their procedure. The Inquisitors were then allowed to give a sermon in the church, in which they demanded a profession of faith from all males over the age of 14 and all females over 12. Those who did not or could not profess were automatically suspect and would be the first to be questioned. The congregation was obliged to swear an oath against heresy and ordered to go to confession three times a year. The Inquisitors then asked them to think about their past actions and make confidential statements the following week, either confessing to their own sins, or denouncing their neighbour. Cathars who voluntarily confessed were resettled in areas where no heresy was known, and had to wear two yellow crosses sewn onto their clothes, which identified them as former heretics. Known or suspected heretics who hadn't confessed voluntarily within this first week were issued a summons to appear before the Inquisitors immediately. Heresy, in the eyes of the Inquisition, included being a Perfect, sheltering them, 'adoring' them (i.e., performing the *melioramentum*), witnessing a 'heretication' (i.e., a *consolamentum*), and failing to report others. The Inquisitors needed at least two witnesses to convict someone; witnesses' names were always withheld, making it all the easier to accuse an enemy – who may have been a perfectly upstanding citizen – of heresy. In a gruesome and deliberately shocking ploy, the Inquisitors did not just restrict the search for heretics among the living. If people named dead relatives as heretics, their bodies were dug up and burnt. If the denounced deceased had any living relatives, their homes and possessions were taken, and they were forced to wear the yellow crosses to acknowledge their relatives' heresy.

Once the Inquisition had names, it was merciless in its pursuit of suspected heretics. The Inquisitors had the power to search a house, and burn down any building where heretics were known to have hidden. Anyone caught in possession of an Old or New Testament was seen as suspicious, and the sick and dying were watched closely lest 'wicked and abominable things'[76] occur (i.e., they receive the *consolamentum*). Once a suspect was caught, they were bombarded with questions: Have they seen a heretic or been acquainted with one? How many times have they seen them? Where did they see them? Who was with the heretics? Has the suspect admitted heretics into their home? If so, who brought them? How many times did the heretics visit? Where did they go after they left? Did the suspect adore them? Did the suspect see others adore the heretics? Did the suspect witness an heretication? If so, what were the names of the people at the ceremony? If the person was hereticated on their deathbed, where were they buried? If they recovered, where are they now?[77]

The ruthless fanaticism with which the Inquisitors carried out their duties is illustrated by the fate of an old woman in Toulouse. A Cathar Believer, she wanted to receive the *consolamentum* while she was still able. On her deathbed, her family sent out for a Perfect to come and administer the sacrament. A Perfect was located, ministered to the woman and left before the Inquisitors got wind of his presence in the woman's house. However, they did get to hear of the deathbed *consolamentum*, and went to question the woman. Under the impression she was talking to the Cathar bishop, Guilhabert de Castres, she described her faith in detail. This was enough. Despite the fact that she only had a matter of hours left to live, she was taken out, still in her bed, and burnt.

Despite the power they wielded, the Inquisition met fierce – and frequently violent – resistance. In Albi, the Inquisitor Arnold Catalan's assistants were too frightened to enter the cemetery to dig up the body of a woman who had been posthumously accused of heresy. Incensed, Arnold went to the cemetery himself with several of the bishop's staff in tow. He broke the topsoil, intending to leave the actual digging to the bishop's underlings, but before any further work could be done, a mob set upon Arnold and nearly beat him to death. They were only prevented from throwing the body of the unconscious Inquisitor into the River Tarn by the intervention of an armed delegation from the bishop. While Arnold was recovering in the safety of the cathedral, the mob outside shouted for his head to be cut off, put in a sack and then thrown into the river. Without even waiting to recover from his ordeal, Arnold excommunicated the entire town. There were similar incidents elsewhere. At Cordes two agents of the Inquisitor were thrown to their deaths down a well; in Moissac, while the Inquisitors Peter Seila and William Arnold were burning heretics, Cistercian monks were hiding them; in Narbonne, when Dominicans attempted to arrest a suspect an argument broke out that led to the sacking of the Dominican convent there.

Raymond VII was initially supportive – he was not in a position to be otherwise – but in 1235 a chance arose to fight back. Relations between the papacy and the Holy Roman Emperor, Frederick II, were becoming increasingly strained. Indeed, they had never been good: one of Gregory's first actions as pontiff had been to excommunicate Frederick for dallying over his crusading commitments. When Frederick did finally set off for the Sixth Crusade in 1227, Gregory excommunicated him again for going on Crusade while excommunicated. Raymond offered to intervene in the Languedoc on Gregory's behalf if the Inquisitors could be made to show more restraint. Gregory agreed, and tried to curb the Inquisition's most fanatical agents in the Languedoc. Seeing that they had regained some ground, the Toulousains began to resist even more. Cathars and their sympathisers were hidden or whisked out of town. Matters escalated until, in October, the Inquisitors were thrown out of Toulouse by a jeering mob, which pelted them with stones and excrement. Realising he needed Raymond as an ally, the pope could do little more than write the count an angry letter, and installed a Franciscan friar, Stephen of St Thibéry, as the new Inquisitor, hoping that the Franciscans' reputation for being more humane than their Dominican brothers might go some way to alleviate tensions.

Unfortunately, the move backfired as Stephen proved to be as fanatical as any Dominican.

The Inquisition did score some successes, however. Two Perfect who had converted to Catholicism, Raymond Gros and William of Soler, provided dozens of names, and also told the Inquisitors that the Perfect had adopted a number of strategies to help them escape detection. Some male and female Perfect travelled in pairs, pretending to be married couples; some deliberately ate meat in public; others swapped their black robes for blue or dark green ones. Such ploys were seen as evidence of the cunning and deceit of heretics, despite the fact that it was the Catholic Church that made such cunning and deceit necessary.

The Trencavel and St Gilles Revolts

As the Inquisition continued to go about its detested business, discontent grew. Raymond Trencavel, son of Raymond Roger, attempted to capitalise on the ill-will shown towards the agents of the Church. From exile in Aragon, he assembled an army which in 1240 besieged his ancestral seat of Carcassonne. After a tense and bloody stand-off that lasted for over a month, the two sides agreed a truce. Raymond would never regain his birthright, but was at least still alive.

Raymond VII had played no part in the Trencavel revolt, but, with the death of Gregory VII the following year, he saw a chance to intervene militarily. The papacy was in no position to stop him, as Gregory's successor, Celestine IV, was pope for only 17 days, and, due to Frederick II's attacks on Rome, it wasn't until June 1243 that his successor, Innocent IV, was elected. By the spring of 1242, Raymond had persuaded King

Henry III of England and Hugh de Lusignan, the most powerful baron in Aquitaine, to join forces with him.

As if to announce the start of the revolt, the Inquisitors Stephen of St Thibéry and William Arnold were murdered on 28 May at Avignonet by a small group of Cathar supporters from Montségur. News of the incident spread quickly, and was greeted with enthusiasm; one country priest even rang the bell of his church to celebrate the deaths of the Inquisitors. Within days, Raymond's forces struck, taking French possessions and Dominican properties with decisive ease. By late summer, it looked as if the coup would be successful, but then things began to go wrong: Henry landed with a force that was too small to do anything other than get itself wiped out, which it successfully managed to do in an engagement with French forces near Bordeaux. Among Henry's knights was Simon de Montfort the younger, whose changing of sides was on a par with that of Arnold Amaury, and would no doubt have made his father turn in his grave. Hugh of Lusignan, suddenly fearing he might be on the losing side, joined the French. But the death knell was sounded by none other than Roger Bernard of Foix. Despite his family's long history of pro southern, pro-Cathar, anti-French activism, Roger Bernard too felt that the revolt was doomed, and negotiated a separate peace with the French. Raymond VII realised that all was lost, and he too came to terms in January 1243. It was the end of the St Gilles family's power in the Languedoc, and everyone knew it.

The Fall of Montségur

With Raymond now a spent force, the Church had only one

place left to tackle that openly defied them: the Pyrenean fortress of Montségur, the so-called 'Synagogue of Satan' that had been a Cathar stronghold ever since the days of Innocent's 'peace and faith' campaign. At a council at Béziers in the spring of 1243, it was decided that action against Montségur had to be taken. By the end of May, an army led by Hugh of Arcis, the royal seneschal in Carcassonne, was in place at the foot of Montségur, but given the fortress's reputation for impregnability, they knew they would be in for a long wait.

Montségur had been refortified in 1204 by Raymond of Pereille. He was a Believer, and both his mother and mother-in-law were Perfect. The castle had been a refuge for Cathars during the Albigensian Crusade, and when the Inquisition began its work, Guilhabert de Castres, the Cathar bishop of Toulouse, approached Raymond with the request that the castle become the centre of the faith. By the time Guilhabert died (of natural causes) around 1240, it was home to around 200 Perfect, overseen by Guilhabert's successor, Bertrand Marty. They were protected by a garrison of 98 knights, under Peter Roger of Mirepoix, whom Raymond of Pereille had appointed co-lord of Montségur at some point prior to 1240. Raymond had guessed – rightly – that the community would need armed protection as the noose of the Inquisition tightened around the Languedoc. Peter Roger, who was from a family of Cathar Believers, had more in common with the bellicose Paulicians than the pacifist Perfect: he was not averse to armed robbery in order to keep the community fed, and had been the instigator of the assassinations at Avignonet. During its heyday, Montségur had been busy as a centre of both intense devotion and industry. Pilgrims travelled great distances to hear the Perfect preach, to be consoled, or simply to spend time in retreat. When not busy with tending to the needs of the Believers, the Perfect helped support the community by working as weavers (a craft long associated with heresy), blacksmiths, chandlers, doctors and herbalists. By the time the siege began, the total number of people living there – including the knights' families – was somewhere in the region of 400.

Hugh of Arcis did not have enough men to encircle the two-mile base of the mountain, and in such craggy terrain siege engines were useless. Hugh had no choice but to try to take the fortress by direct assault. His forces made numerous attempts to scale the peak, but each time were driven back by arrows and other missiles lobbed over Montségur's ramparts by Peter Roger and his men. The months dragged on wearily and, by Christmas, Hugh's army was becoming disillusioned. He needed a breakthrough if there was any chance of raising morale. He ordered an attack on the bastion that sat atop the Roc de la Tour, a needle of rock at the eastern end of the summit. The men climbed the Roc by night, and caught the garrison at the top by surprise. The defenders were all killed. When daylight came, the royal troops looked down in horror at the sheer face they had scaled, swearing they could never have made the ascent by day. Nevertheless, it gave the royal forces a strong foothold just a few hundred yards from the main castle itself, and work began immediately on winching up catapults and mangonels. Bombardment began immediately.

Inside the walls of Montségur, the atmosphere of devotion intensified. While Peter Roger's men returned fire on the French troops, who were edging ever nearer from their foothold at the Roc, Bertrand Marty and Raymond Agulher, the

Cathar bishop of the Razès, attended the spiritual needs of both the garrison and the non-combatants. A messenger arrived to say that Raymond VII might intervene to lift the siege. Rumour had it that Frederick II was also planning a rescue mission to liberate Montségur. The weeks dragged on, but no one came. Finally, on 2 March 1244, Peter Roger walked out to announce the surrender of the fortress to Hugh of Arcis. The victors were lenient with their terms: everyone could go free, provided they allowed themselves to be questioned by the Inquisition, and swore an oath of loyalty to the Church. Past crimes, including the assassinations at Avignonet, were forgiven. For the Perfect, the choice was as stark as it had been for their forebears at Minerve and Lavaur: renounce Catharism, or burn. They had two weeks to think about it.

For the Perfect, it was no choice at all. Not one of their 200-strong number was willing to recant. They spent the two weeks of the truce distributing their goods to their families and followers. Peter Roger was given 50 doublets that the Perfect had made to sell or give away as he saw fit. The atmosphere inside the castle during this period must have been indescribable, a sorrow touched with the joy in knowing that, for the Perfect, their journey through the vale of tears that is the material world would soon be over. On the final Sunday of the truce, 21 Believers – some of whom had originally gone to Montségur merely as mercenaries to help Peter Roger defend the castle, and all of whom had the option of going free – asked to be given the *consolamentum*. They knew that in doing so, they were giving themselves up to the pyres already being built at the foot of the mountain. If there is anything in the entire history of Catharism that illustrates the appeal and power of the faith, it is this extraordinary moment. All of them were consoled.

At first light on Wednesday, 16 March 1244, Montségur was evacuated. Peter Roger and his knights and their families went free, watching as the Perfect were lashed together on the pyres. They were from all walks of life: Corba of Pereille and her daughter Esclarmonde were nobles (as well as being Raymond of Pereille's wife and daughter), while William Garnier was, if not a peasant, certainly a man of humbler means than the Pereilles. The 21 last-minute converts were also among their number, as were Bertrand Marty and Raymond Agulher. Hugh of Arcis and Peter Amiel, the Archbishop of Narbonne, looked on as the pyres were lit. The site of the burnings is still known to this day as the Field of the Cremated.

The Inquisition after Montségur

With the last major redoubt of Catharism gone, Perfect and Believers found themselves in a world with little shelter and fewer protectors. No one was safe, as Peter Garcias found out to his cost in Toulouse during Lent 1247. His relative, William, a Franciscan, had invited him to their convent in order to discuss issues of faith and doctrine. Naturally, Peter had no qualms about telling William about his Cathar faith; after all, William was family. Peter railed against the Church of Rome, declaring that it was a 'harlot who gives poison', while the law of Moses was 'nothing but shadow and vanity'.[78] Peter was too trusting: in a scene reminiscent of the exposing of Basil the Physician, a curtain was pulled back to reveal that Peter's testimony had been carefully transcribed by a team of secretaries. Peter was handed over to the Inquisition.

William Garcias was not the only person to betray his family to the Inquisitors. A former Cathar Perfect, Sicard of Lunel, denounced scores of his former associates and supporters 'whether they had offered him a bed for the night or given him a jar of honey.'[79] The list of people he denounced included his parents. Sicard's treachery was amply rewarded by the Church, and he survived well into old age.

These two examples were but among many. The Languedoc in the years immediately after the fall of Montségur was subject to inquisitorial scrutiny of proto-Stalinist proportions. Heading this clampdown on the thirteenth-century equivalent of thoughtcrime were Bernard of Caux and John of St Pierre. Over 5,000 depositions survive, but this is only a fraction of what was actually taken down at the time. As Malcolm Lambert notes, Bernard, John and their brethren were attempting to build 'a total, all-embracing picture'[80] of Cathar belief, practices and support in the areas in which they operated.

For the Cathars, being caught presented a major dilemma: the Perfect were forbidden to lie or to swear oaths. Whatever they did, they would be compromising their beliefs. Some chose to tell the truth, and thereby implicate other Perfect, Believers and supporters, while others either lied or gave away as little information as possible. Others opted for collaboration, and became double agents, continuing to live as Cathar Believers and receiving the fugitive Perfect into their homes, and then reporting them. Collaboration, however, was risky, as there were frequent reprisals against turncoats. One such was Arnold Pradier, who had been a Perfect during the de Montfort years, but later converted to Catholicism along with his wife (who had also been a Perfect) and began naming names. The Inquisition installed them in a safe house, the Château Narbonnais in Toulouse, where they lived well at the Church's expense.

Although resistance continued – at Castelbon, the Inquisitor was poisoned and the castle attacked – there was ultimately little people could do. The Inquisition became a fact of life, 'an entrenched institution rather than a single, unrepeated ordeal.'[81] If people were suspected of giving false or incomplete testimony, they were hauled back in front of the Inquisitors to be reinterrogated, regardless of whether they were high-born or peasant. Faced with such intensive action, most nobility realised there was no point anymore in trying to oppose the Church; even Raymond VII began to persecute suspected heretics, burning 80 at Agen in June 1249.

The Fall of Quéribus

While the Inquisition was doing its inexorable work, there was still one Cathar castle attempting to hold out against all the odds. The eleventh-century castle of Quéribus sat on a rocky outcrop high in the Corbières. Like Montségur, its remoteness and the difficulty of the terrain protected it from the attentions of northern forces. The castle had been sheltering fugitive Cathars for years, ever since Oliver Termes regained lordship over his ancestral lands at Termes after the death of Alan of Roucy, the northern Crusader who had been given the fief by Simon de Montfort, in the early 1220s. Oliver had played a part in the Trencavel and St Gilles revolts of the early 1240s, which had led to the loss of his castle at Aguilar, to the north-east of Quéribus, and to his excommunication. The Church trusted him about as much as it had Raymond VI of Toulouse. Like Raymond

VI, he was undeterred by excommunication, and together with his co-lord, Chabert of Barbéra, he continued to shelter Cathars at Quéribus until Oliver was forced to submit to King Louis IX in 1247. Oliver redeemed himself sufficiently during the Seventh Crusade (1249–54) that some of his possessions, including Aguilar, were returned to him. However, upon his return from the Crusade in 1255, he was forced into one final act of betrayal: he had to ambush and hand over Chabert of Barbéra to the Inquisition.

Unlike the fall of Montségur, the fall of Quéribus is still shrouded in mystery. It is not known how many Cathars were in residence at the time, and neither is it certain whether the castle fell by force or surrender. But fall it did, in August 1255. Oliver managed to save the life of Chabert through negotiation, and all the Cathars in the castle managed to escape. During the winter of 1255–56 Peter of Auteuil, Louis's seneschal in Carcassonne, took over the castle, and also the neighbouring castle of Puylaurens, which was also known to be sympathetic to the Cathars. There were now no walls the Good Christians could hide in safety behind. The Cathar church was driven underground.

5

The Autier Revival

Catharism was, in the years after the fall of Quéribus, a chimerical presence. According to the testimony of Stéphanie de Châteauverdun, a noble and Cathar Perfect from the Sabartès, what top-level Cathars remained were living in the mountains. William Prunel was one such Perfect, whose career stretched from around 1258 until 1283. Despite the tireless efforts of the Inquisition, the one thing that was hardest to eradicate from the Languedoc was the deep roots that Catharism had put down. Even after all the atrocities and hardships that the area had suffered over several decades, people still seemed unwilling to give up completely on the old religion. Evidence to support this comes from the fact that William once spent a month in Toulouse; he was recognised as a Cathar, but no one betrayed him. He continued to spread the faith, and was known to have nobility and clergy amongst his flock. Another Perfect, William Pagès, was also active during the same period, although he had managed to survive by spending time in Lombardy.

Apart from the willingness – or otherwise, as in the case of William Prunel – to betray a known Cathar, the Inquisition faced other problems during this period. Foremost among them was the crucial relationship between Inquisitors, bishops and royal officers. Although the machinery of repression was generally efficient, its effectiveness did vary from area to area. In Narbonne, for instance, hostility towards the Inquisitors had diminished to such an extent by the early 1260s that they were called on to arbitrate on the town's behalf in a secular dispute with Béziers. In Albi, however, the bishop and the Inquisitors were at loggerheads with royal officials for years over the issue of confiscating the property of convicted Cathars: the bishop favoured leniency to prevent families from being bankrupted, and was, remarkably, supported by the Inquisitors. Royal officials were attacked by crowds of locals; in return, the bishop's bastides – small fortified new towns – were pillaged by royal forces.

Matters deteriorated during the last two decades of the thirteenth century, with complaints against the Inquisitors rising. The Inquisition hit back, accusing royal officials of complicity with heretics: in the 50 years before 1275, there were only two such complaints, but between 1275 and 1306 there were thirty.[82] Things were further complicated by the relationship – not always harmonious – between the French king, Philip IV, and the papacy. Philip took sides against the Inquisitors. As a result of these tensions, arrests for heresy in the period 1297–1300 were largely of a political nature. Once the pope, Boniface VIII, died in 1303, Philip withdrew his support and the Inquisitors got back to work relatively unhampered. As they did so, something quite unexpected happened: there was a Cathar revival.

Peter Autier

Peter Autier was from the small town of Ax-les-Thermes, up-country from Foix. He was born around 1240, and had made a comfortable life for himself as a notary. Notaries drafted legal documents – wills, contracts and the like – and were one of the pillars of mediaeval society. Peter had a wife, a mistress and families with both women, a fact which did not harm his good social standing. During the 1270s, the family firm had done work for Roger Bernard III of Foix, and had gone on to do more state work, which had increased the firm's status and purse. Then in 1296, all that changed.

One day, Peter was reading a book. He showed it to his younger brother William, and asked him what he thought. William replied, 'It seems to me that we have lost our souls.' Peter nodded his assent and said, 'Let us go therefore, brother, and seek the salvation of our souls.'[83] What book they were reading remains unknown, but René Weis conjectures that it 'would almost certainly have been St John's gospel.'[84] They decided to go to Lombardy – where there were still active Cathar communities – to receive the *consolamentum*. There had been a history of Catharism in Peter's family – the father and son Peter and Raymond Autier, who flourished in the 1230s, were probably collateral relatives[85] – but what is remarkable is that Peter knew full well what he was letting himself in for, and that he was prepared to turn his back on a very comfortable existence.

In early October 1296, he and William probably left for Lombardy. There is still a mystery surrounding their departure. Peter was apparently in a great deal of debt to Simon Barre, the hereditary châtelain of Ax. Simon was not above terrorising his debtors and – on occasion – calling for their deaths. In order to repay this debt, Peter Autier sold all his cattle at the Michaelmas fair in Tarascon. After that, it is sheer conjecture: Peter and William left for Lombardy around 4 October. It remains a possibility that the debt was deliberately engineered to make it seem as though Peter was fleeing Ax for financial reasons, rather than spiritual. If rumours of debt – rather than heresy – had spread around Ax, it would have bought the Autier brothers more time to make good their escape into Italy. This is all the more plausible when one considers that Simon Barre had Cathar sympathies.

Peter and William travelled with Bon Guilhem, Peter's illegitimate son, together with Peter de la Sclana, whom one assumes was a close associate of the Autiers. Later, they were joined en route by one of Peter's daughters and her husband. Peter and William received the *consolamentum* from an Italian Perfect in Cuneo, a town in south-west Piedmont, which had been a centre for exiled Languedocian Cathars since the middle of the century. Then, around St Martin's Day (11 November) 1297, Bon Guilhem reappeared in Ax. He informed the Autiers' extensive network of family and supporters that Peter and William had become Perfect in Italy, and wanted to return as soon as it was safe for them to do so.

It was Peter who returned first, reaching Toulouse in the autumn of 1299. That the purpose of his visit was to see a money changer suggests that securing the mission's finances was his priority. For all his careful planning, Peter's cover was blown almost immediately, when he was recognised by Peter, the son of Raymonde de Luzenac, a rich widow whom Peter Autier had attempted to convert to Catharism three years earlier. The young de Luzenac was studying law at the time, and had run up considerable debts. Peter Autier bought the young man's silence by paying off the money de Luzenac owed.

Meanwhile, William reappeared in Tarascon, preparing the

way for the missionary work to begin. While the brothers had been in Lombardy, they had kept in touch with family back home and, by 1300, a wide network of safe houses had been established for the brothers to utilise on their return. During the winter and through into the spring of 1300, William and Peter Raymond of Saint-Papoul, another Perfect, lived in a dovecote that belonged to a family of Cathar Believers. Given the power of the Inquisition, Peter and William would need to mount a commando-style operation if they were to stand even a slim chance of success.

Yet success is precisely what they achieved. The brothers recruited about a dozen others, whom they consoled, to help spread the word. Among their number were Peter Raymond of Saint-Papoul, the weaver Prades Tavernier, Amiel de Perles, Peter's son James, James's friend Pons of Ax and Aude Bourrel, the last known female Perfect. The group relied on the Autier family network for protection and support. Bernard Marty – possibly a relative of the great Cathar bishop Bertrand Marty, who died at Montségur – was a shepherd who frequently acted as a scout and escort for the Perfect (his father owned the dovecote that William and Peter Raymond stayed in), and his older brother Arnold would become one of the Autier Perfect. Martin Francès from Limoux acted as the group's treasurer; his wife was a devout Cathar who would receive the *consolamentum* on her deathbed from Peter Autier. Bertrand of Taix was a minor noble who was also a lifelong Cathar Believer. He frequently supplied the Perfect with gifts, such as the barrel of wine he sent to the Autiers when they returned from Lombardy. He also let them stay on his estates when need arose. Bertrand's wife was a devout Catholic, a fact he never ceased bemoaning. To her credit, she let him continue to support the Autiers and did not betray him. Sybille Baille had a secret room in her house in Ax for the Perfect to hide in, while the de Area brothers at Quié had the equivalent of a priest hole below their grain chest.

Almost as soon as the group began their work in the spring of 1300, they were in danger. They were approached by one William Dejean, who appeared to be a Cathar Believer. After apparently expressing some interest in joining the Autier group, the next day he visited the Dominican convent in Pamiers, offering to betray the Cathars to the Inquisition. What he did not realise was that the friar he spoke to, Raymond de Rodes, was Peter Autier's nephew. Raymond immediately told his brother William, who then told Raymond Autier, the one Autier brother who was not a Cathar. William and Raymond realised that Dejean had to be dealt with at once. He was lured up a mountain pass, where four Believers beat him to a pulp. When questioned, he was able to answer that he had been intending to betray the Autiers to the Inquisition. The four then threw Dejean over the cliff into the ravine below. His body was never recovered.

Inquisitors who later questioned a number of the Cathars' key supporters recalled Peter Autier's sometimes idiosyncratic brand of teaching. He was a radical dualist who took Docetism a step further. While Docetic doctrine ordinarily denies Christ's corporeality, Peter also believed that the Virgin Mary was similarly non-physical, being instead a manifestation of the will to do good. He also believed that, for a woman to enter heaven, her soul would first have to become that of a man. Despite this strain of misogyny, Peter was a popular and successful preacher, not without humour. He once remarked that crossing oneself was only good for batting away flies, while on another occasion he advised Believers that, if they had to cross themselves while in the company of Catholics, they should mentally say to themselves 'Here is the forehead and here is the beard, here is one ear and here is the other.'[86] On the Eucharist, he pointed out that Christ's body would need to be as big as a mountain if it were to feed all the communicants. Furthermore, if Transubstantiation was a reality, priests and Believers would, after digesting, have God in their bowels, a God who would inevitably be expelled from the body on their next visit to the water closet.

The Endura

Autier Catharism was different from that of earlier eras in that it was operating clandestinely. There was no hierarchy: Peter Autier was not a bishop or a deacon, he was simply a Perfect, and that was enough. His Perfect travelled at night, being guided by the likes of Bernard Marty over the mountainous terrain of the Sabartès. If they travelled by day, they did so disguised as merchants or pedlars (Peter and William travelled back from their consoling in Lombardy posing as knife salesmen). They slept and taught in cellars, attics, dovecotes, sheds and grain silos.

The group's principal activity was in administering the *consolamentum* to the dying. In a society deeply damaged by the Inquisition, where husbands concealed their Cathar beliefs from their wives and vice versa, the visits of the Perfect had to be discreet and expertly timed. If they arrived too soon, they would not have the time to wait until the consoled Believer died, while obviously if they arrived too late, there was nothing they could do. Some of the consolings were remarkably audacious. A woman by the name of Gentille d'Ascou was dying in the hospital at Ax in September 1301. By the time William Autier arrived late one evening, she was too weak to walk or sit upright unsupported. As the hospital was also an unofficial brothel – prostitutes plied their trade at the town's nearby thermal spa pool – William had no choice but to risk carrying out the *consolamentum* in the field at the back of the hospital.

Three years later, William performed perhaps the most celebrated of these derring-do *consolamentums* for Peter de Gaillac's mother Gaillarde in Tarascon. Around 50 people came to Gaillarde's bedside to pay their last respects. As William needed total privacy for the *consolamentum*, Peter's aunt Esclarmonde urged him to find some excuse to get the well-wishers out of the house while there was still time to console Gaillarde. Peter announced that the heat (it was August) was proving too much for his mother, and that she would be much more comfortable if everyone left. The ruse worked, and only Esclarmonde and Peter's grandmother Alissende were left alone in the room with the dying woman. They then locked the door from the inside, and Esclarmonde entered the house next door via a secret passageway where William Autier was waiting. She gave him her cloak and cape to wear, and William entered the house disguised as Esclarmonde and performed the *consolamentum*.

In the first of these cases, the *consolamentum* was followed by a practice called the *endura*. This required the newly consoled Cathar to refrain from taking anything except cold water while they lingered in this world. As fear of betrayal meant that the Perfect could not remain with the consoled to ensure that they did not deviate from the stipulated diet of a Perfect, the *endura* was the practical answer that ensured the newly Perfected Cathar would remain true to the articles of the faith. Taking nothing but cold water, Gentille d'Ascou lasted for another six days after her *consolamentum*. Guillemette Faure, a woman from Montaillou, lasted 15 days in *endura* when she was on her deathbed in December 1299. The longest *endura* known was that of a woman from Coustaussa, who took 12 weeks to die. (However, this seems to be an extreme case of a woman who wanted to die, and used the *endura* as a means of starving herself to death.)[87]

Enduras did not always go according to plan, however. When Bernard Marty fell sick with a fever in early 1300, he was consoled and then put into the *endura*. After three days he couldn't stand it anymore and demanded to eat something; he recovered to become one of the Perfect's most loyal allies.[88] In 1302, Sybille Autier lay dying in her house in Ax. Her mother was with her, as were William, her Catholic brother-in-law, and Esclarmonde, the wife of Raymond Autier. Sybille's husband, who was not a Cathar, was not aware of his wife's intentions to be consoled, and was asleep in his bed. William lingered on at the dying woman's bedside a trifle too long for comfort, and Esclarmonde became desperate to get rid of him so that William Autier — who was waiting in a house nearby — could come in and perform the *consolamentum*. She asked the Catholic William to walk her home, which he agreed to do. As soon as they were gone, Sybille's mother hurriedly went to fetch William Autier. By the time the Perfect got to Sybille's bedside, she was delirious and was incapable of making the necessary responses that the *consolamentum* required. William said that he would perform the *consolamentum* if she regained her faculties, but she didn't and died unconsoled. It is possible that the Catholic brother-in-law suspected what the women were planning, and deliberately stayed at the dying woman's bedside long enough to ensure that a consoling would not be possible.

As not all the Perfect agreed with Peter Autier on doctrinal matters, so the same held true with the *consolamentum*. Unlike William Autier, Prades Tavernier performed a number of consolings for Believers who were not capable of the response, either due to the fact that they were too ill, or, in one case, because the person to be consoled was a baby only several months old. Once Prades, who was evidently a bit of a soft touch and could often be persuaded to console people who were in no fit state to receive the sacrament, had left the house, the baby's mother almost immediately invalidated the consoling by giving her baby the breast. The little girl, Jacqueline, lived for another year, but died without being reconsoled.

Geoffrey d'Ablis and Bernard Gui

Things began to go wrong for the Autier group in 1305. Upon his release from prison, William Peyre, a trusted confidant and Believer, wanted money to pay off a debt he had run up while incarcerated. For reasons unknown, the Autiers refused him the money, and Peyre lured James Autier and Prades Tavernier to Limoux on the pretext of performing a *consolamentum*. It was a trap, and the two Perfect were arrested. It could have spelt the immediate end for the Autier network, but James and Prades managed to escape almost immediately. Nevertheless, the damage was done. Peyre told the Inquisition everything he knew about the group's operations, and how widespread it had by then become – at least 1,000 Believers were part of the Autier flock, scattered over 125 locations.[89] But the Autiers still had a great deal of support; Peyre's brother was murdered in Carcassonne in retaliation for his treachery, and Peyre was still living under the equivalent of a witness protection programme as late as 1321.

A much greater challenge was to come from the Inquisition. Either side of the arrests, two men were appointed to run the Inquisition in the Languedoc who would go down in history as two of the most able churchmen ever to hold down the job: Geoffrey d'Ablis and Bernard Gui, presiding over Carcassonne and Toulouse respectively. The confessions they extracted from suspects – and those extracted by James Fournier, bishop of Pamiers from 1317 – are so detailed that they are the best record we have of any period of Catharism. Despite their fearsome reputation, d'Ablis and Gui received appeals for clemency, and often granted it. Of Gui's 930 convictions, only 42 were death sentences.[90] Perhaps the most notable example of the efficiency of the new Inquisitors occurred at Montaillou. On 8 September 1308, the whole village was arrested on suspicion of heresy.

The Last Perfect

With the renewed vigour inspired by Geoffrey d'Ablis and Bernard Gui, the Inquisition eventually caught up with nearly all of the Autier Perfect. They were arrested, interrogated and burnt during 1309–10.[91] Sans Mercadier, a young weaver who had only been consoled in 1309, was not caught but committed suicide in despair. Peter Autier spent eight months in prison before being burnt on 9 April 1310 in Toulouse. Now in his late sixties, he remained defiant to the very end. As he was being tied to the stake, he asked to be allowed to preach to the crowd which had come to watch him die; Peter announced that he would convert all those present to Catharism. His request was denied, and, with his passing, there remained only one Perfect still at large in the Languedoc.

William Bélibaste was from the Corbières. Sometime before Easter 1305, he killed a fellow shepherd. Later that year, shortly before James Autier and Prades Tavernier were arrested in Limoux, he had met the Perfect Philip d'Aylarac while the latter was travelling by night and wanted to take refuge in William's sheepfold. The meeting was to change William's life. He joined the Autier network, and was consoled. In 1307, he and Philip d'Aylarac were imprisoned in Carcassonne on suspicion of being heretics, but managed to escape in September of that year; they evaded their gaolers by hiding all day in a stream. Bélibaste seems to have then crossed over the border into Catalonia. After the Autier movement was effectively destroyed in the arrests and burnings of 1309–10, he remained in exile, where he tended to a group of Believers who had fled from the Languedoc.

Bélibaste's ministry was an unusual one. He kept a mistress in the shape of Raymonde Piquier, but outwardly kept up the pretence of the celibacy required by the *consolamentum*. In 1319, he arranged for Raymonde to marry Peter Maury, a shepherd and Cathar Believer, in an attempt to fool people into thinking that Peter was the father of the child that Raymonde was carrying. Several days after the marriage, Raymonde and Peter were divorced and she moved back in with Bélibaste. Despite his shortcomings, however, Bélibaste was an inspired preacher who conscientiously guided his diminished flock as best he could. He urged his followers never to give in to despair, stressed the need to love one another and praised the good God who waited for them all in the true world, the immaterial world of light. As Stephen O'Shea notes, 'Bélibaste's sermons were remembered for years'[92] by his followers.

The group was troubled by the arrival of a newcomer, Arnold Sicre, in 1317. His credentials seemed respectable enough. He had come from Ax-les-Thermes, where his mother Sybille and his brother – Pons of Ax, one of the Autier Perfect – had been burnt by the Inquisition. He asked for instruction in the faith, but not all of Bélibaste's group were convinced he was genuine; his father was not a Cathar and had helped organise the raid on Montaillou. Nevertheless, despite these reservations, Sicre became part of the group and found work locally as a cobbler. After a year with the group, Arnold informed Bélibaste that he wanted to search for his rich aunt and younger sister, who lived, so he said, somewhere in the Pallars valley, a part of Aragon that bordered on the county of Foix. He made two trips north in search of his family, each time returning with money that he said his aunt wanted Bélibaste to have to fund his teaching. Finally, he announced that his sister, Raymonde, wanted to marry. Bélibaste decided that she would make a fine wife for one of the group, Arnold, Peter Maury's brother; the prospect of having a rich benefactress also appealed.

Bélibaste set off with Sicre to meet the aunt and the sister sometime around the middle of March 1321. It was a sting. Once they reached Tírvia, which was within Fuxian jurisdiction,

Bélibaste was arrested. Arnold Sicre explained that he had done it because he wanted to reclaim his mother's house, which had been forfeited when she had been burnt. The aunt and nubile sister had never existed: during his absences, Sicre had instead been visiting James Fournier, who was spearheading a fresh wave of Inquisitorial proceedings. Sicre's treachery did not stop there. Once Bélibaste had been put into custody, he immediately put himself into the *endura*, hoping to starve himself to death before he could be burnt. Sicre convinced the Perfect that he was sorry for his actions, and told Bélibaste that he had devised an escape plan, which could only be carried out if Bélibaste were fit. He abandoned his fast. Sicre had been lying again – there was no plan, no escape. Had Dante been a Cathar,[93] one could easily imagine Sicre being placed in one of the lower circles of hell for his treachery. Sicre had his mother's house restored to him, and continued to betray other Cathars to the Inquisition. No record of Bélibaste's trial survives, and he was burnt in the small town of Villerouge-Termenès.

Montaillou

James Fournier, meanwhile, was continuing to interrogate afresh people who had been questioned ten years earlier by Geoffrey d'Ablis (who had died in 1316). Fournier was a much more thorough inquisitor, and managed to extract a wealth of new information. In particular, he found that the situation in Montaillou was much graver than had originally been thought. Almost everyone there had been, or still was, a Cathar, which instigated a fresh wave of arrests. A number of factors had allowed Catharism almost to take over the entire village. There was no lord to keep an eye on things, as he had died in 1299, and his widow, Béatrice de Planisolles, seems to have been converted – at least for a time – to Catharism by Peter Clergue, the village's rector. Although a Cathar, Clergue was still outwardly a Catholic priest, saying mass, hearing confessions, performing baptisms and funerals. He was also notoriously promiscuous, bedding many of the women in the village, including Béatrice, with whom he once had sex in the church. Peter's brother Bernard was the village's bayle – effectively an agent for the local count of Foix – and was also a Cathar. Together the two men effectively controlled the village, and had the power to keep unwelcome visitors out.

The early 1320s were a legalistic marathon, with Fournier sentencing hundreds of people. Béatrice de Planisolles was sent to prison, but her sentence was later commuted to the wearing of yellow crosses. Various members of Bélibaste's group were jailed, including Peter Maury and his brother John, who were sentenced to 'perpetual prison' on 12 August 1324. Peter Clergue, the randy rector of Montaillou, died before he could be sentenced. On 16 January 1329, he was pronounced a heretic, and his remains were dug up and burnt.

It was the end of Catharism in the Languedoc. What Believers there were left had all been forced to confess and recant. There were to be no more consolings, or 'holy baptisms', as the ritual of the *consolamentum* phrased it, a tradition which, the Cathars believed, had come down to them 'from the time of the apostles until this time and it has passed from Good Men to Good Men until the present moment, and it will continue to do so until the end of the world.' Now that there were no more Good Men left, it seemed that the end of the world had truly come.

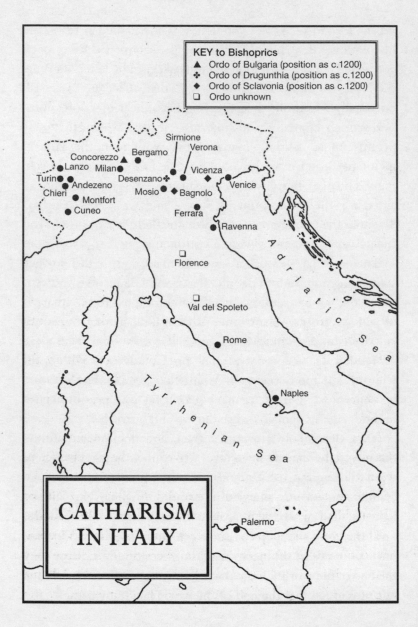

KEY to Bishoprics
- ▲ Ordo of Bulgaria (position as c.1200)
- ✤ Ordo of Drugunthia (position as c.1200)
- ◆ Ordo of Sclavonia (position as c.1200)
- ❑ Ordo unknown

Sirmione
Verona
Concorezzo
Bergamo
Lanzo
Milan
Turin
Vicenza
Desenzano
Andezeno
Chieri
Mosio
Bagnolo
Venice
Montfort
Cuneo
Ferrara
Ravenna
Adriatic Sea
Florence
Val del Spoleto
Rome
Tyrrhenian Sea
Naples

CATHARISM IN ITALY

Palermo

6

Italy and Bosnia

Thirteenth-Century Italian Catharism

Italian Catharism entered the thirteenth century as a fractured church, with Concorezzo and Desenzano being respectively the bastions of the moderate and absolute schools. The *ordo* of other churches, such as those at Florence and the Val del Spoleto, remains unknown. Like the Languedoc, the political situation helped nurture the growth of Catharism, but, unlike the south of France, opposition did not generally come from Crusaders but from reforming movements that originated both within and without the Church. From within, the way was led by St Francis of Assisi who, while not mentioning the Cathars – or Patarenes as they were frequently known in Italy – by name, stressed the importance of closely examining the beliefs of potential new recruits to the Franciscan order. He wrote of the importance of regular attendance at both church and confession, and of the need to respect priests. He also stressed the physical reality of Christ's birth, which went against the Docetism of the Cathars.

There were also popular preachers such as John of Vicenza, who commanded the attention of huge crowds every time they gave a sermon. In John's case, it led to the rise of the Alleluia movement, a popular, if short-lived, phenomenon in the tradition of the pro-reform Pataria of Gregory VII's day, and John presided over the mass burning of 200 heretics – mainly Cathars and Waldensians – in Verona in August 1233. John's success led to the founding of a number of lay confraternities, such as that of St Maria of Misericord in Bergamo, which were intended for people who wanted to further their spiritual practice without having to become a monk or nun. Its members swore to adhere to certain rules, such as the refusal to shed blood, to bear weapons and to refrain from an unethical way of life. They also actively worked towards the repression of heresy.

While the various movements acted as outlets for people who were dissatisfied with traditional forms of religiosity, conflict between the papacy and the empire created space in which Catharism could flourish. The reign of Emperor Frederick II (1220–50) saw these confrontations reach their zenith, and Italian politics came to be dominated by two factions, the pro-papal Guelphs, and the pro-imperial Ghibellines. Frederick did little to encourage the persecution of heretics, and the papacy, keen to gain allies in the key cities of Lombardy, did not press the heresy issue. Also, many cities, wishing to maintain their independence, did not enforce anti-heresy legislation, not because they were especially sympathetic to groups such as the Cathars or the Waldensians, but because any attempt to persecute heretics would have necessarily led to a greater role for the Church, thereby decreasing the cities' autonomy. Cathars were relatively free to go about their business under the protection of the Ghibelline nobility, and in Lombardy, a Languedocian Cathar church in exile flourished.

Cathar Writings

Very few Cathar tracts have come down to us. Most of the surviving works come from Italy, where literacy levels were generally higher than in the Languedoc, and where the controversy between various Cathar factions encouraged polemicism. Moreover, Italy's geographical closeness to the Balkans meant that books arriving from the east, such as the Bogomil *Secret Supper* and *The Vision of Isaiah*, would generally first appear in the west on the Italian peninsula. These two works were known in the west by the end of the twelfth century. *The Secret Supper* elucidates the Bogomil/Cathar creation myth, in which Satan is cast out of heaven for wishing to be greater than God. Satan pretended to repent, at which God forgave him and let him do what he wanted. With his new-found freedom, Satan created the world of matter, and formed human beings from the primordial clay. Each soul was a trapped angel from heaven. Satan then convinced humanity that he was the one true god, an action which caused the real god to send Christ – a spirit who entered Mary through her ear – in order to alert humanity to the ways of the devil and to announce the existence of the true god. *The Vision of Isaiah* was accepted by both the moderate and absolute schools, as it 'showed a material world and a firmament riven by the battle between Satanic and Godly forces.'[94]

The most important surviving Cathar tract is *The Book of the Two Principles*, which was written in the 1240s, probably by John of Lugio, a Cathar from the Albanensian[95] school, which was part of the absolutist church of Desenzano. It is 'the most decisive evidence that the Cathars were evolving their own ideas about the nature of Dualism',[96] and were not content simply to recycle Bogomil material. The *Book of the Two Principles* is a sustained polemic against the moderate school, whom the author regards as almost no better than Catholics (who also come in for attack during the course of the argument). The work makes a case for there being two coeternal principles of good and evil, each of which created their own spheres – heaven and the material world respectively. The true god cannot be the author of evil. The verse in the Gospel of John which states 'All things were made by it [the Word of God], and without it, was made nothing'[97] was interpreted as meaning that 'nothing' – i.e., the material world – was made by Satan. The true world was the domain of the real creator god, which was not a world of matter, but a higher world that obeyed its own laws.

Also extant is a very late tract – possibly from the third quarter of the fourteenth century – called *The Vindication of the Church of God*. It presents the Cathars 'as a persecuted and martyred church, suffering before the appearance of the Antichrist and the Last Judgment.'[98] It states that 'this Church of God has received such power from our Lord Jesus Christ that sins are pardoned by its prayer', that 'this Church refrains from adultery', that 'this Church refrains from theft', concluding that 'this Church keeps and observes all the commandments of the law of life', in sharp contrast to 'the wicked Roman Church'.[99]

The Decline of Italian Catharism

The pro-imperial Ghibelline party received a major setback with the death of Emperor Frederick II on 13 December 1250. His son Conrad IV continued the struggle, but the papacy emerged victorious with the capture and execution of Frederick's grandson Conradin in 1268, who was the last of the Hohenstaufen rulers. With the loss of their main ally, the Ghibellines went into decline, and the Cathars they were protecting found themselves vulnerable to the attentions of the Inquisition. After the murder of the Inquisitor and former Cathar Peter of Verona by Cathar-hired assassins in 1252, pope Innocent IV wasted no time using it to the Church's advantage: Peter was canonised as St Peter Martyr, and Innocent authorised the use of torture during inquisitorial procedure.

The intensification of the Inquisition's efforts drove many Cathars underground, or into living double lives. Perhaps the most extraordinary case of this is that of Armanno Pungilupo of Ferrara. He was thought of as a pious Catholic who was famed for his good works and, after his death on 10 January 1268, was buried in the cathedral. His saintly reputation persisted, and miracles were reported around his tomb. After much rooting around by the Inquisition, it emerged that Armanno had been not just a Cathar Believer, but had been a Perfect for the last 20 years of his life. He even survived a brush with the Inquisition in 1254, who tortured him, made him swear loyalty to the Catholic Church and threatened to impose a heavy fine on him if he was caught engaging in heretical practices in the future. Armanno agreed, and promptly carried on as before. Even one of the so-called miracles at his tomb, that of a mute who suddenly regained the power of speech, was found to have been faked by a Cathar intent on lampooning the Church's cult of miracles. Eventually, the Inquisition prevailed, and Armanno's remains were dug up and burnt in 1301, and his ashes thrown into the River Po.

By far the most serious loss the Italian Cathars sustained was the fall in 1276 of the castle at Sirmione, which stood on a peninsula extending into Lake Garda. Sirmione was the Italian Montségur, and had been home to various exiled Cathars, including the last active bishop of the Northern French Cathar church, and also the last Cathar bishop of Toulouse, Bernard Oliba. In February 1278, all 200 Sirmionese Perfect were burnt in the amphitheatre at Verona.

Brute force and mass murder, however, were not the sole reasons for Catharism's decline in Italy. As Malcolm Lambert notes, 'alternative paths to salvation had opened up',[100] and people were able to express their dissatisfaction with the Church in other ways, not just by becoming Cathars. Groups such as the lay confraternities certainly played a large part in this, as did the enormous success of the Franciscans. Unlike the Languedoc, where Catharism was extinguished in a Church-sponsored holocaust that ended with the Inquisition of James Fournier and the burning of William Bélibaste, Catharism in Italy faded away slowly. The last known Cathar bishop was arrested in 1321, and the last known Cathar in Florence was hauled up before the Inquisition in 1342. By this date, the only remaining Cathars existed in secretive mountain communities in the Alps, where, for several more decades, they managed to elude the long arm of the Inquisition.

The Last Cathars

The last Cathars haunted the remote valleys of the Piedmont. An almost invisible presence, they co-existed with groups of fugitive Waldensians, only occasionally breaking their cover to murder a priest who tipped off the Inquisition about their location in 1332, and two Inquisitors, who met the same fate in 1365 and 1374. Once enemies, the Waldensians and the Cathars were now forced together by circumstance, and 'came to see persecution as a special mark of the true church.'[101] The persecution continued in the form of sporadic military action: the French mounted an expedition against the Waldensians in the Dauphiné in 1375, but on the Lombard side of the Alps, the use of force remained a logistical and political impossibility. Slowly but surely, the Inquisition closed in on the last remaining communities. Cathar sentiments were discovered in 1373 in the Val di Lanzo, while Antonio di Settimo di Savigliano's inquisition of 1387–9 uncovered the last two major Cathars: Antonio di Galosna and Jacob Bech.

Antonio di Galosna had been a Franciscan in Chieri, near Turin, but in 1362 had been introduced to the heresy in a house in Andezeno, a small town to the north-east of Chieri. The ceremony he participated in seems to have been part Waldensian and part Cathar, which indicates that, by this very late date, the Piedmont Cathars were practising a hybrid form of the faith. Galosna related to the Inquisition that he had renounced his belief in the incarnation of Christ and the sacraments of the Catholic Church. That a syncretistic or degenerate form of Catharism was being preached at Andezeno is evident in that, after visiting his teacher several times, Antonio was ritually struck on the head with a sword in order to induct him into the heresy.[102] He was then given dualist instruction, in which God was extolled as the creator of heaven, but not of earth; the latter was apparently created by a fearsome dragon, which exercised more power in the earthly realm than the true god.[103] A further teacher, Martin de Presbitero, had appointed Antonio to hear confessions, and was apparently present at two degenerate *consolamentums*, in which the consoled, rather than being put into the *endura*, were suffocated with pillows. Under torture, Antonio related stories of orgies presided over by a woman called Bilia la Castagna, who made a magic potion out of toad droppings and pubic hair to ensure that the novice would never leave the sect. This was undoubtedly untrue, as belief in sexual deviation had been a standard part of heresy accusations ever since Orléans in 1022, and it is fairly certain that Antonio was merely telling the Inquisitors what they wanted to hear.

Jacob Bech's confession, however, makes it clear that not all of the Piedmont Cathars entertained notions about dragons – he was taught the more orthodox Cathar view that material creation was under the sway of Satan, and he also told the Inquisition of links between the Piedmont Cathars and *Ecclesia Sclavoniae*, which were apparently still active at that time. Indeed, Bech claimed to have been converted by two Italian Cathars and a third individual from 'Sclavonia', and that the Balkan heretics had their own pope.[104] Before that, Bech had been a member of various heretical groups, including the Apostolics, and his travels had taken him as far as Rome and Avignon. At one point, he had even been given money by a well-wisher to cross the Adriatic to seek further instruction from Balkan heretics, but was unable to make the crossing due to inclement weather. In time, Bech himself began to gather disciples, and at Castagnole he was honoured with a feast. When he was asked about the *consolamentum*, Bech corroborated Galosna with reference to the euthanasia by suffocation, but added that the consoled had another option, that of a complete three-day fast, in which they could not even take that staple of the *endura*, cold water. If they survived, they would become Perfect, but would have to give all their worldly goods to the one who had consoled them. Bech told the Inquisition that he had settled in Chieri, where moderate Catharism was rife, and that a number of other Cathars had gone from there to Bosnia for further instruction.[105] Both Galosna and Bech were burnt, and Catharism in the west effectively died with them.

In 1412, the Inquisition returned to Chieri and dug up 15 dead Cathars – some of whom had been named by Bech as having journeyed to Bosnia – and burnt their remains. There were apparently no Cathars left alive, although the Inquisition acknowledged that the heresy was still rife across the Adriatic.

The Enigma of the Bosnian Church

Bosnia had always had a reputation for heresy. As early as 1203, Innocent III had urged the king of Hungary – the Church's only real ally in eastern Europe and the Balkans – to mount a campaign against the heretics there. The Ban – or ruler – of Bosnia, Kulin, was thought to be a heretic, as were 10,000 of his subjects. At length, Innocent's chaplain, John de Casamaris, was sent to investigate. Ban Kulin rejected all accusations of heresy, and pointed out to John that he had just built a church that celebrated a recent military victory. However, Christianity in Bosnia was underdeveloped, and it is possible that Ban Kulin was not aware of where orthodoxy ended and heresy began. As a precaution, seven senior leaders from various monastic communities submitted to Roman rule at Bilino Polje on 8 April

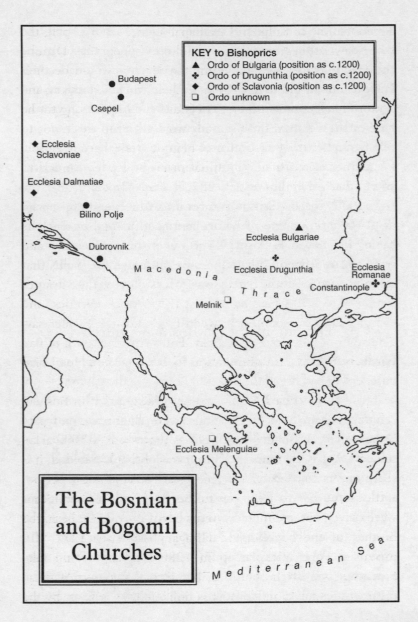

KEY to Bishoprics
▲ Ordo of Bulgaria (position as c.1200)
✤ Ordo of Drugunthia (position as c.1200)
◆ Ordo of Sclavonia (position as c.1200)
□ Ordo unknown

Budapest

Csepel

◆ Ecclesia
Sclavoniae

Ecclesia Dalmatiae
◆

Bilino Polje

Dubrovnik

M a c e d o n i a

Ecclesia Bulgariae ▲

Ecclesia Drugunthia ✤

Ecclesia
Romanae

Constantinople ✤

T h r a c e

Melnik □

Ecclesia Melenguiae □

The Bosnian
and Bogomil
Churches

M e d i t e r r a n e a n   S e a

1203 before Ban Kulin and the papal legate. On 30 April, the ceremony was repeated on an island off Csepel in the Danube south of Budapest, only this time the seven priors made their submission in front of Ban Kulin, Emeric, king of Hungary, and senior Hungarian churchmen. In addition to submitting to the rule of the Church, the Bosnians were made to agree not to receive anyone they suspected of being a 'Manichaean'.

Despite this, the heresy situation in Bosnia continued to worry successive popes. In 1232, it was discovered that the Catholic bishop of Bosnia was an uneducated simoniac who not only did not know how to baptise, but also lived in the same village as heretics.[106] He was removed from office and replaced by a Dominican. It became clear to Gregory IX that a military solution was necessary. He appointed the king of Hungary to lead Crusades against the Bosnian heretics, and campaigns were mounted between 1234 and 1246, which saw a number of heretics being burnt. Following the death of Ban Ninoslav around 1250, Bosnia was forced to accept Hungarian rule.

This seems to have been a major turning point in Bosnian religious affairs. While the Crusades were attempts to extirpate heresy, they ultimately backfired, as it was under Hungarian suzerainty that the Bosnian Church was probably founded; it is still a matter for debate, and records are scarce for the period. Little seems to have been done to check heresy; the Dominicans were driven out and their convents burnt down. Elisabeth, the mother of the boy king of Hungary, Ladislas (1272–90), promised Pope Nicholas III in 1280 that she would take measures against the heretics, but it is not known if these measures achieved anything. It is unlikely they did, as, by the time the Bosnian Church emerged again into the historical record, around 1322, it was condemned by both Rome and the Serbian Orthodox Church as heretical.

The precise nature of the Bosnian Church's heresy remains a matter for speculation. That its members were known as Patarenes – the name for Cathars in Italy – suggests a Catharist orientation. Furthermore, the Church used a ritual that was very similar to the *consolamentum* and included the giveaway phrase 'supersubstantial bread' in the Lord's Prayer, a further strong suggestion that the Bosnian Church was either Cathar, semi-Cathar or at least tolerated Cathar practices within it.

In 1325, Pope John XXII (1316–34) exhorted a number of leaders to take action against the Bosnian Church, as 'many heretics' were flooding into Bosnia. His successor knew all about heresy, as he was none other than the bishop of Pamiers, James Fournier, who ruled as Benedict II (1334–42), but even he was unable to get a Crusade in motion. The most headway that the Catholic Church was able to make was in the sending of a Franciscan mission to Bosnia, but Stephen Kotromani, Ban 1318–53, remained tolerant of the Bosnian Church, and there were no persecutions. He remained on good terms with the Franciscans, and converted to Catholicism. Heretics remained unpersecuted under Stephen's successor, his nephew, Tvrtko I (1353–91), so much so that the Franciscans complained that 'Patarenes' were allowed into church when they said mass, and the support for the heretics was so great that the Franciscans almost had to practise their religion in secret.

Heretics long remained in positions of prominence in Bosnia, and were even sent on diplomatic missions, such as those to Dubrovnik – then an independent republic – in the first half of the fifteenth century. (Indeed, a merchant from Dubrovnik noted in 1458 that the Bosnians 'follow Manichee customs'.[107]) The last great *gosti* – or elder – of the Bosnian Church, Radin, enjoyed a long and successful parallel career as a diplomat, serving both the Bosnian monarchy and Dubrovnik. When he drew up his will in 1466, he drew sharp distinction between members of the Bosnian Church and Catholics, although that did not stop him bequeathing money to the latter.

The increasing threat from the Ottoman Turks led the Bosnian king, Stephen Thomas (1443–61), to appeal to the west for help. To increase his chances of receiving support, he converted to Catholicism and began to persecute the Bosnian Church, a move that made him extremely unpopular with his subjects. Members of the Church were offered the choice of conversion or exile. Some of Radin's community were given asylum in Dubrovnik and Venice, while others chose to defy their king and collaborate with the Ottomans. Bosnia fell to the Ottoman Turks in 1463, but the fate of those members of the Bosnian Church who did not go into exile remains obscure. They are traditionally thought to have converted to Islam, although there are reports of Bogomils, Patarencs and Manichaeans in Bosnia well into the nineteenth century; the last known report dates from 1867.[108] It is perhaps fitting that the Great Heresy, which emerged seemingly from nowhere during the tenth century, should have an equally obscure and mysterious end.

7

The Cathar Treasure

Since their demise, many legends have circulated about the Cathars, usually centring around the so-called Cathar Treasure, and their relationship with the Troubadours and the Knights Templar. Much of this is the result of the romanticisation of Catharism by nineteenth- and twentieth-century writers such as Napoléon Peyrat and Déodat Roché, whose work we will examine later in this chapter. However, such legends have actually been circulating since at least the 1320s,[109] and deserve to be briefly outlined below, as they have played a crucial role in shaping the mystique surrounding the Cathars, which has in turn helped retain the interest and imagination of the public, speculative historians and mystics for generations.

The Cathars and the Holy Grail

Perhaps the most enduring myth about the Cathars is that they possessed the Holy Grail, the cup said to have been used by Christ at the Last Supper, which also caught drops of his blood at the Crucifixion. Although, as will be noted below, modern writers have managed to get a great deal of mileage out of the Grail, they did not invent the Cathar/Grail myth. It originated in the twelfth and thirteenth centuries, while Catharism was still very much alive.

These Grail stories began in the city of Troyes, courtesy of the quill of Chrétien de Troyes; his *Conte del Graal,* written around 1180, is the first mediaeval Grail narrative.[110] It concerns the attempts of King Arthur's knights to attain the Grail, but, due to Chrétien's death, it breaks off before the quest is completed. The story was picked up by Robert de Boron, whose *Joseph of Arimathea* (c. 1200) Christianises the story, and then by Wolfram von Eschenbach. Wolfram's greatest work is *Parzival* (c. 1200–1210), which is frequently read as an allegory of spiritual development, betraying the influence of the east (Wolfram was thought to have gone on Crusade) and also of alchemy. In Wolfram's poem, the Grail castle is called Munsalvaesche, which some (see below) have taken as a coded reference to Montségur, as both names have the same meaning, 'safe, or secure, mountain.' Wolfram continued to write about the Grail in the unfinished *Titurel*, which was fleshed out and completed by Albrecht von Scharfenberg. Albrecht's poem, *Jüngerer Titurel* (c. 1272), seems to be making a direct link between the Grail and the Cathars, when he names the first king of the Holy Grail 'Perilla'. This is the Latinised version of the name of Montségur's lord, Raymond Pereille. Why does Albrecht make this link? Coincidence? Literary fashion? Or did he know some secret about the Cathars, whose existence he wanted to hint at in the poem?

Speculative writers argue there was indeed a secret: the Cathars possessed the Grail, and draw attention to one dramatic event that seems to corroborate this. During the siege of Montségur, either just before the two-week truce in March

1244, or during it, four Cathars scaled down the mountain in the dead of night, carrying with them a 'treasure', which was then either hidden in a nearby cave, given to other Cathar groups, or entrusted to the Knights Templar. Whatever this treasure was, it had to be portable enough to be carried down a precipitous mountainside, and a chalice would certainly fit the bill. Montségur's sergeant, Imbert of Salles, however, told the Inquisition that the Cathar Treasure was merely money and precious stones.[111] But stories about secret hordes of Cathar treasure persisted. Some held that the treasure was simply vast amounts of money, hidden at various locations, while others argued that the treasure could be nothing so mundane or vulgar, that it comprised secret texts or sacred documents, containing divine wisdom and revelatory truths. Conveniently for the myth, the four Cathars disappeared from history, taking the treasure with them.

Although the Grail is usually depicted as a cup (sometimes a platter), Wolfram's grail, in *Parzival*, was said to be a stone, which recalls the Philosopher's Stone in alchemy. However, there have been alternative interpretations of the Grail. One of the more controversial suggestions is that the Grail is, in fact, the womb of Mary Magdalene, which was seen as the chalice that caught Christ's blood not on Calvary but after the wedding at Cana, at which Jesus and the Magdalene became man and wife, after which they raised a family. The Magdalene hypothesis suggests that the Holy Grail, which is *san graal* in French, is, in fact, a misspelling of *sang real*, the holy blood, meaning the bloodline of Jesus and the Magdalene. This theory has most famously been explored in Michael Baigent, Richard Leigh and Henry Lincoln's classic *The Holy Blood and the Holy Grail*. More recently, it has been the subject of Dan Brown's global bestseller *The Da Vinci Code*. However, the idea that Jesus married Mary Magdalene does not originate with Baigent, Leigh and Lincoln: one of the Cathars' inner teachings, which was only passed on to the Perfect, was that the Magdalene was Jesus's wife.[112] This is puzzling, to say the least, as the Cathars despised marriage. Furthermore, it was not a belief inherited from the Bogomils. It is possible, in believing that Jesus and Mary Magdalene were married, that the Cathars were reflecting a popular Languedocian tradition, but we cannot be certain.

The Troubadours and the Knights Templar

The two groups with whom the Cathars are most often associated are the Troubadours and the Knights Templar, both of whom had a very strong presence in the Languedoc during the thirteenth century. The Troubadours were itinerant poets writing in Occitan who flourished between the eleventh and thirteenth centuries. In Germany, they had fellow travellers in the shape of the Minnesingers, of whom Wolfram von Eschenbach was one. The Troubadours' main themes were chivalry and courtly love, in which the virtues of a particular lady would be extolled by the poet. Sometimes these were literal love songs, often addressed to a woman who was unattainable, while other Troubadour poems and songs were in fact allegories of spiritual development, and betray an awareness of the Divine Feminine. Among the most celebrated Troubadours were Peter Vidal, William Figueira and Jaufré Rudel. In the Languedoc, they enjoyed the protection of the same families which protected the Cathars. At least one

Troubadour, William de Durfort, was known to be a Cathar; no doubt there were others. The concept of the Divine Feminine suggests another link between the two movements: the Perfect, upon being consoled, were given the title of *Theotokos*, which means 'God-Bearer', an assignation usually associated with the Virgin Mary.

The Knights Templar were the most powerful military religious order of their day, and were major landowners in the Languedoc. While theories suggesting that the Cathar treasure – whatever its nature – was entrusted to the Templars remain fanciful, there are a number of more definite links between the heretics and the soldier-monks. One of the Templars' great Grand Masters, Bertrand de Blancfort, was said to have come from a Cathar family, and during the Albigensian Crusade, the Templars welcomed fugitive Cathars into the order. In some Templar preceptories in the Languedoc, Cathars outnumbered Catholics. Furthermore, the Templars refused to participate in the Albigensian Crusade. There could have been a number of reasons for this. They had a great deal of support in the Languedoc, so any military intervention there would have been politically disastrous for the Order, and, towards the end of the de Montfort years, they were actively involved in the Fifth Crusade (1217–21), in which they played a decisive role. However, one cannot help but wonder if certain elements within the Temple remained sympathetic to the Cathars, a sympathy rendered all the more plausible by the fact that the Templars were themselves viciously suppressed between 1307 and 1312, on charges of heresy, blasphemy and sodomy – charges that had been formerly levelled against the Good Christians.[113]

Modern Cathars

The romanticisation of the Cathars began with the Languedocian writer Napoléon Peyrat (1809–81). Despite being a priest himself, he was also a member of an anticlerical group known as the Priest Eaters, and launched numerous attacks on what he saw as the reactionary nature of the Catholic Church. To bolster his arguments, he invoked the name of the Cathars, whom he regarded as southern martyrs. His mammoth *History of the Albigensians*, published in the 1870s, took frequent liberties with the known facts in the name of mythologising the Cathars and denigrating the Church. Montségur became a kind of Camelot, full of wonders that were still awaiting discovery, and Peyrat was convinced that the Cathar Treasure was a cache of sacred texts hidden in caves at nearby Lombrives. Peyrat also wrote of a community of Cathars taking shelter in the caves after the fall of Montségur, who lived there until they were discovered by northern troops, who walled them up alive in the cave. Despite the high drama of this tragic story, there is no evidence that it ever happened. Like so much in Peyrat's work, it is the product of imagination, rather than historical record. For Peyrat, the Cathars, in their anti-papal stance, were forerunners of Protestantism and also foreshadowed the French Republic.

Peyrat's mythologised, semi-fictional Cathars had a big impact on the likes of the Félibrige, a group of scholars which were keen to preserve works written in Occitan. Underneath this goal lay a separatist movement, that wanted to restore Languedocian independence and identity. Peyrat was regarded as something of a guru, and the group began to produce its own

Cathar theories, which tended to view the Cathars as occult initiates. The Cathar Treasure thus became a repository of ancient wisdom, with the Cathars being descended from the Druids, Hindus or Buddhists, while Montségur was interpreted as a solar temple. (Again, like Peyrat's Cathars-in-a-cave story, this is pure fiction.)

Déodat Roché (1877–1978), another southern self-styled Cathar expert, published a number of pro-Cathar works, including *L'Église romane et les Cathares albigeois* (1937) and *Le Catharisme* (1938). In 1948, he began publishing a magazine, *Cahiers d'Études Cathares*, and two years later, founded a group, the Société du Souvenir et des Études Cathares. During the 1930s, he headed a loose-knit group that included the novelist Maurice Magre (1877–1941) and the philosopher Simone Weil (1909–43), both of whom wrote pro-Cathar polemics. Magre famously referred to the Perfect as 'the Buddhists of the West', while Weil saw them – along with the Gnostics and the Manichaeans – as being one of the manifestations of the perennial philosophy; what was most needed, she felt, was a revival of Cathar spirituality and the simple lifestyles of the Perfect.

A third figure who came into Roché's orbit was the young German writer Otto Rahn (1904–39). In his first book, *The Crusade Against the Grail* (1933), Rahn interprets Wolfram von Eschenbach's *Parzival* as a thinly disguised account of the Albigensian Crusade. In Rahn's reading of Wolfram, the Cathar Treasure is the Holy Grail itself, with Montségur as the Grail castle Munsalvaesche, and the martyred Raymond-Roger Trencavel as Parzival. In his next book, *The Court of Lucifer* (1937), Rahn compared the struggles of the Cathars against the

Crusaders with those of Hitler to establish the Thousand Year Reich, seeing the Cathars as good Aryans who opposed not just Rome but also Judaism. It comes as no surprise to learn that, by this time, Rahn was working for Himmler, and writing what Himmler wanted to hear. Subsequently, myths have grown up around Rahn, depicting him as a German Indiana Jones who actually found the Grail and took it back to Germany, where it was hidden in the Bavarian Alps shortly before the end of the war. Other accounts of dubious provenance have the Nazi theorist Alfred Rosenberg flying over Montségur on 16 March 1944, the 700th anniversary of the citadel's fall, as a mark of respect for the Good Christians, while Hitler himself was said to belong to a neo-Cathar group. With Otto Rahn, we see the Cathars claimed, not for Languedocian nationalism, but for the perverted Germanic myth-making of the Nazis.

A far more benign form of neo-Catharism is to be found in the work of the English psychiatrist Arthur Guirdham (1905–92). In the 1960s, a certain Mrs Smith, one of Guirdham's patients, began telling him about her previous life as a Cathar in thirteenth-century Languedoc. Initially sceptical, Guirdham began to investigate her claims, and wrote to Jean Duvernoy, one of Catharism's leading historians. Much to Guirdham's surprise, Duvernoy corroborated the details of Mrs Smith's story. The resultant book, *The Cathars and Reincarnation* (1970), details Guirdham's further discoveries, including the possibility that he himself was a reincarnated Cathar. The story was continued in *We Are One Another* (1974) and *The Lake and the Castle* (1976). Guirdham's *The Great Heresy* (1977) is a brief history of the movement, and included in its later chapters revelations dictated to him by disembodied Cathars, covering such topics as the healing power of crystals, the aura, the emanatory powers of touch and the true nature of alchemy. The Perfect, according to Guirdham, were well-versed in such things during their earthly existence.

The Persecuting Society

The Cathars emerged at a time of profound change in Europe. The historian R I Moore has argued that western society formed its institutions through the persecution of heretics and others in the thirteenth century.[114] Furthermore, definitions of heresy played a large part in shaping the concept of witchcraft, which greatly aided the persecution and execution of thousands of innocent people – predominantly women – during the Witch Craze of the sixteenth and seventeenth centuries.

It is perhaps the Cathars' quest for an authentic spirituality that makes their story still relevant. Their belief that they – and not the Church – were the real Christians calls to mind Dostoyevsky's parable of the Grand Inquisitor, in which Christ returns to earth, specifically Seville, during the height of the Spanish Inquisition. He is immediately arrested as a heretic, and questioned by the aged Grand Inquisitor. The old man prefers the safety and power the Church offers to Christ's simple message. He tells Christ 'If anyone has ever deserved our fires, it is Thou. To-morrow I shall burn Thee.' He waits for Christ to respond: ' "He saw that the Prisoner had listened intently all the time, looking gently in his face and evidently not wishing to reply. The old man longed for him to say something, however bitter and terrible. But He suddenly approached the old man in silence and softly kissed him on his bloodless aged lips. That was all his answer. The old man shuddered. His lips moved. He went to the door, opened it, and said to Him: 'Go, and come no more ... come not at all, never, never!' And he let Him out into the dark alleys of the town. The Prisoner went away."'[115]

The Cathars' claim to be part of an authentic apostolic tradition dating back to the time of Christ cannot be proved, only inferred. The Catholic Church's claim to descend from Peter is also historically unverifiable. Something that perhaps finds in the Cathars' favour is one of the Dead Sea Scrolls, only made public for the first time in 1991. The end of the *Damascus Document — The Foundations of Righteousness: An Excommunication Text* — appears to show the excommunication of Paul from the Christian community.[116] If this were indeed the case, then it would problematise the Catholic Church's claim to be God's vicars on earth, as most of the major forms of organised Christianity owe far more to the teachings of Paul than they do to those of Jesus. The Church obviously feels that publication of the text has not damaged its position, and in March 2000, Pope John Paul II issued an apology for the Crusades. Many felt that the statement did not go far enough in offering rapprochement to the Arab world. No mention was made of the Albigensian Crusade. It remains unlikely that the papacy will ever apologise for the genocide it committed against the Good Christians.

Perhaps the real Cathar treasure is to be found in their stress on simplicity, equality, non-violence, work and love. By not building churches, they necessarily brought divinity into the domestic sphere, suggesting that, for the Cathars, every moment of every day could be used to deepen one's spiritual life. Maurice Magre's belief that they were the Buddhists of Europe is arguably not too far wide of the mark. Given that the Church – both the Catholic Church and the religious right in America – seems to be as conservative and exclusive as it ever was, the Cathars' message is perhaps as relevant now as it was in the Languedoc of the twelfth and thirteenth centuries, as Simone Weil argued.

Perhaps the real Cathar treasure was indeed smuggled out of Montségur that night in March 1244. But it was not a cup or text: if the Cathars scaling down the mountain that night were Perfect, then they themselves were the real treasure, a reminder and example to everyone who has been moved by the Cathar story down the centuries: a reminder to stand defiant in the face of persecution; to do the work of the Good Christians, the work of Amor, not Roma; to become living icons.

Endnotes

Epigraphs:
'Throughout human history...' Michael Baigent and Richard Leigh, *The Inquisition*, p.148.
'Bishop Fulk...' Malcolm Lambert, *The Cathars*, p.138.
'Salvation is better achieved...' Emmanuel Le Roy Ladurie, *Montaillou*. Quoted in Baigent and Leigh, p.7.

[1] Lambert, *The Cathars*, p.103.

[2] The Waldensians, also known as the Poor Men of Lyons, followed lives of Apostolic poverty. They were denounced as heretics in the bull *Ad abolendam* issued by Pope Celestine III in 1184, a move that only served to radicalise them further.

[3] 2 Timothy 2:19: 'The Lord knoweth them that are his.' (Tyndale translation).

[4] O'Shea, *The Perfect Heresy*, p.86.

[5] Yuri Stoyanov, *The Other God*, p.2. The leading orientalist of his time, Hyde (1636–1703) was chief librarian at the Bodleian Library in Oxford. He coined the word 'cuneiform' and investigated the origins of chess.

[6] Ugo Bianchi, *Il Dualismo Religioso* (Rome, 1958), quoted in Stoyanov, pp.4–5.

[7] Mary Boyce, *Zoroastrians: Their Religious Beliefs and Practices* (Routledge and Kegan Paul, 1979), p.1.

[8] Mary Boyce, p.29.

[9] Another development during the Achaemenid era was an offshoot of Zoroastrianism, Zurvanism, which held that both Ohrmazd and Ahriman were the twin offspring of the god of time and destiny, Zurvan.

[10] René Descartes (1596–1650) argued for an irreconcilable split between the mind and the body. He is widely seen as one of the founders of modern philosophy.

[11] This suggests a possible Egyptian influence on Orphism. In some versions of the myth, it is Osiris who opposes Seth, not Horus, and in these, Seth first drowns Osiris and then dismembers the body; Osiris is later resurrected.

[12] Originally, the word *Satan* – meaning 'adversary' in Hebrew – was titular, referring to any angel who happened to be acting in this capacity. See Elaine Pagels, *The Origin of Satan*, p.39. This leads to an interesting parallel, in that the word *Christ* is also titular (meaning the Annointed).

[13] In Genesis, Eve was tempted by the Serpent, not Satan.

[14] Indeed, Satan steps into God's shoes in more ways than one: in earlier (in terms of writing) Old Testament literature, it is always God whom – in His wrath – is humanity's adversary.

[15] Some versions have it as seven years of famine.

[16] See, for instance, Elaine Pagels, *The Origin of Satan*, p.42ff.

[17] Quoted in Pagels, pp.60–61.

[18] Matt 16.18: 'And so I tell you, Peter: you are a rock, and on this rock foundation I will build my church.'

[19] See, for instance, Robert Eisenman's *James the Brother of Jesus*.

[20] A N Wilson, *Paul: The Mind of the Apostle*, p.258.

[21] Michael Baigent and Richard Leigh in *The Dead Sea Scrolls Deception*, p.266.

22 Thomas Jefferson, from a letter to W. Short published in *The Great Thoughts* by George Sildes (Ballantine Books, 1985) p.208.

23 The fact that Constantine's mother, the Empress Helena of Constantinople (c.255–c.330), was already a devout Christian may have had some bearing on her son's willingness to convert. She is credited with finding the True Cross, whose location was revealed to her in a dream.

24 This clause was actually added at the Second Ecumenical Council – Nicaea being the first – in 381.

25 In fact, they were followers of the Roman presbyter Novatius, and were also known as Novatians.

26 At approximately the same time, other forms of non-dualist heresy – such as Pelagianism, which denied Original Sin – were quashed, in addition to other forms of Christianity that diverged from Rome, such as the Celtic and Nestorian churches. A case could be made for the former being the original form of Christianity in Europe, while the latter – despite persecution – persists to this day.

27 Nina G. Garsoïan, *The Paulicians*, p.112ff, pp.186–231.

28 For a fuller treatment of this period, see Stoyanov, pp.139–58.

29 Stoyanov, p.170.

30 For possible heretical leanings in Gerbert, see Runciman, *The Medieval Manichee*, p.117. Gerbert was also suspected of having made an oracular head, of having learnt astrology and alchemy from the Moors and of founding a papal school of magic.

31 Stoyanov, p.185.

32 For a brief summary of the origins of the devil as a black man,

see Lois Martin, *The History of Witchcraft*, p.18.

[33] Lambert, p.13.

[34] Cited in Lambert, p.14.

[35] Eberwin of Steinfeld, *Epistola ad S. Bernardum*, quoted in Wakefield and Evans, *Heresies of the High Middle Ages*, pp.126–32.

[36] Wakefield and Evans, pp.126–32.

[37] Cited in Lambert, p.20. It is possible that what the *Annals* are recording is, in fact, the Cologne episode erroneously transposed to Bonn.

[38] Lambert, p.21.

[39] Good News Bible translation.

[40] St Bernard of Clairvaux, *Eighty-Six Sermons*, ed. Eales, p.407, quoted in Lambert, p.40.

[41] R I Moore, *The Origins of European Dissent*, p.113.

[42] Alan of Lille, *De fide Catholica*, quoted in Lambert, p.43.

[43] The Cathars did not reject the whole of the Old Testament, and continued to hold the Psalms, Job and the prophets in high regard.

[44] Lavatorial anecdotes, Lambert p.29.

[45] This memorable description of the Perfect comes from Fichtenau, quoted in Lambert, p.30.

[46] *Consolamentum* ceremony, Wakefield and Evans, p.467.

[47] 'Publicans' was one of the numerous names used at the time to denote dualist heretics. It probably derives from 'popelican'. The jury is still out on whether the Publicans were Cathars. Even if they weren't, the two groups certainly had much in common.

[48] Some authorities, e.g., Malcolm Barber, believe the St Félix meeting took place a few years later, between 1174–77.

Some believe it didn't happen at all, although the weight of scholarly opinion is firmly on the side of its taking place. See O'Shea, p.272.

49 Lambert, pp.45–6.

50 Heinrich Fichtenau, *Heretics and Scholars in the High Middle Ages 1000–1200*, pp.152–3.

51 Lambert, p.34.

52 Bernard Hamilton, 'Wisdom from the East', in *Heresy and Literacy, 1000–1530*, ed. P. Biller and A. Hudson (Cambridge, 1994), pp.39–40.

53 C. Thouzellier, 'Hérésie et croisade au XIIe siècle', *Revue d'histoire ecclésiastique*, 49 (1954) pp.855–72, cited in Stoyanov p.191.

54 Lambert, p.33.

55 O'Shea, p.45.

56 O'Shea, p.51.

57 O'Shea, p.53.

58 The debates at Béziers and Carcassonne lasted 15 days apiece. The proceedings at Montréal were recorded by scribes, but their chronicles seem to have been lost during the Albigensian Crusade.

59 O'Shea, p.65.

60 The moment was witnessed by the ambassador of Navarre. Lambert, p.102.

61 It remains a possibility that Peter was killed by one of Raymond's enemies in the south, hoping that the count of Toulouse would get the blame for the assassination. Alternatively, Peter could have even been killed by a Catholic agent hoping to provoke Innocent into action. If this was the case, then he certainly succeeded.

[62] O'Shea, p.87.

[63] English writer (fl.1200). It was while working as a clerk in the household of William of Champagne, cardinal archbishop of Rheims (d. 1202), that Gervase accused a young girl of heresy when she rejected his advances. For maintaining her dignity, she was burnt at the stake.

[64] Cited in Lambert, p.103.

[65] The scene is recorded in *The Song of the Cathar Wars*.

[66] Barber, p.133. I am indebted to Barber for most of the information in this section.

[67] Barber, p.133.

[68] Barber, p.135.

[69] Gaucelm (1204–c.1220) and his successor Guilhabert de Castres (c.1220–c.1241).

[70] Barber, p.135.

[71] *The Song of the Cathar Wars*, p.176.

[72] Discussed in Claire Dutton, *Aspects of the Institutional History of the Albigensian Crusades 1198–1229*, PhD Dissertation, Royal Holloway and Bedford New College, University of London, 1993.

[73] Joseph R. Strayer, *The Albigensian Crusades*, p.i.

[74] Lambert, p.123.

[75] This is an extraordinary admission for an orthodox apologist. Such claims were later made against such scholars as Cornelius Agrippa, and were widely associated with witchcraft.

[76] Quotation of unknown provenance, presumably taken from an instruction manual for Inquisitors, cited in Barber, p.145.

[77] Bernard Gui, *Practica Inquisitionis*, cited in Zoé Oldenbourg's *Massacre at Montségur*, pp.307–8.

[78] Lambert, p.160.

[79] O'Shea, p.229.

[80] Lambert, p.217.

[81] Abels and Harrison, *Medieval Studies*, 41, p.223.

[82] Lambert, p.226.

[83] René Weis, *The Yellow Cross*, p.77.

[84] Weis, p.77.

[85] Weis, p.73.

[86] Lambert, p.249. It should be noted that not all of Peter's fellow Perfect agreed with him on the subjects of Mary and women. While James Autier agreed with his father on many things, William Autier believed Mary to be a real woman, while Bélibaste believed in Purgatory and a form of the Trinity, making him ironically quite close to Catholicism. Lambert, pp.252–5.

[87] Guillemette Marty was so afraid that the Inquisitors would come and force her to eat during her *endura* that she tried killing herself by drinking poison, then by bleeding and was preparing to stab herself with a shoemaker's sewing needle in the heart when the poison seems to have been finally effective. Weis, p.97.

[88] René Weis notes that 'the *endura* probably saved Bernard's life by starving the fever.' Weis, p.90.

[89] Lambert, p.259. The Autier faithful almost certainly numbered more than 1,000, as several valuable Inquisition registers have not survived.

[90] Barber, pp.196–7.

[91] Philip d'Aylarac seems to have remained at large until 1312. See Weis, p.244.

[92] O'Shea, p.241.

[93] Dante wasn't a Cathar, but he was certainly aware of them,

and was sympathetic to the work of the Troubadours. See William Anderson's *Dante the Maker*.

[94] Barber, p.88.

[95] The group were so-called after a certain brother Albanus, but whether he existed or not is still a matter for debate.

[96] Barber, p.86.

[97] John 1.3–4 (Tyndale translation).

[98] Barber, p.202.

[99] *The Vindication of the Church of God*, quoted by Lambert, p.223.

[100] Lambert, p.289.

[101] Lambert, p.291.

[102] Syncretism had also been a feature of Montalionian Catharism, where villagers entertained magical beliefs as well as those of the Good Christians, such as Béatrice de Planisolles' keeping of her children's umbilical cords. Furthermore, the Black Death (1347–51) would have played a part in removing a number of those Perfect who still remained in the Alps.

[103] Lambert, p.293.

[104] The myth of an heretical Balkan antipope, a sort of Bogomil/Cathar Prester John, was enduring. The heretics arrested at Montforte in 1025 declared that there was an heretical antipope, while Jacob Bech confirmed to the Inquisition in 1387 that the Cathars had their own pope, whom he called their *Papa Major*. Stoyanov, *Hidden Tradition*, pp.190–1.

[105] For Bech's confession, see Lambert, pp.294–5.

[106] Lambert, p.299.

[107] Lambert, p.307.

[108] O'Shea, p.23.

[109] Barber, pp.182–4.

[110] The Grail myths have frequently been seen as the Christianisation of the Celtic myths of the Cauldron of Plenty, although the sudden explosion of Grail romances in the twelfth century seems to be linked to the Crusades and specifically the Knights Templar.

[111] Another puzzle about Montségur is the reason for the two-week truce. Various theories suggest that it was to give the Cathars time to enact a sun-worship ceremony, or to celebrate Easter. Neither can be the case: sun-worship may have gone on in the area around Montségur, but it was probably Bronze Age at the latest, and certainly not during the Cathars' era (although the sun was a symbol used in Manichaeism). The Easter argument likewise does not hold water: the Cathars did not celebrate Easter, and, furthermore, Easter in 1244 fell on 3 April, nearly three weeks after the truce expired.

[112] Stoyanov, *Hidden Tradition*, pp.222–3.

[113] As in the case of the Cathars, charges of devil worship and sexual promiscuity were among the most powerful stock-in-trade accusations against political enemies. Such charges were even levelled against Pope Boniface VIII by King Philip IV of France.

[114] R I Moore, *The Formation of a Persecuting Society*.

[115] Fyodor Dostoyevsky, *The Brothers Karamazov*, Book 5, Chapter 5, translated by Constance Garnett.

[116] Robert Eisenman & Michael Wise, *The Dead Sea Scrolls Uncovered*, pp.212–9; see also Holger Kersten, *Jesus Lived in India*; Baigent and Leigh, *The Dead Sea Scrolls Deception*, pp.286–7.

Appendix I:
Chronology

930s–40s	Emergence of Bogomilism in Bulgaria
c. 970	First anti-Bogomil tract, Cosmas the Priest's *Sermon Against the Heretics*
991	Gerbert d'Aurillac, later Pope Sylvester II, forced to swear his orthodoxy at Rheims
999	Leutard, first known heretic in the west, active in Châlons-sur-Marne
1022	First arrests and executions for heresy in the west, at Orléans
1082	Bogomil missionaries possibly active in Sicily
c.1100	Execution of Bogomil Heresiarch Basil the Physician in Constantinople
1110s–50s	Heretics at large: era of Tanchelm of Antwerp, Arnold of Brescia, Henry of Lausanne *et al.*
1143	First recorded mention of Cathars, burnt at Cologne
1145	St Bernard preaches against Cathars and visits the Languedoc
1163	Council of Tours; Eckbert of Schönau's *Sermones ad Catharos*
1165	Cathar/Catholic debate at Lombers
1167	Cathar Conference at St Félix

1179	Third Lateran Council: use of force against heretics recommended
1181	Short-lived military campaign against Cathars in Lavaur, led by Henri de Marcy
1184	*Ad abolendam* denounces the Cathars and other heretical sects
1198	Accession of Pope Innocent III; Cistercians appointed to preach to heretics in the Languedoc
1199	*Vergentis in senium* equates heresy with treason, and allows heretics' property to be confiscated
1203	April: Bosnian Church forced to swear fealty to Rome
	Arnold Amaury and Peter of Castelnau appointed papal legates in the Languedoc
1204	Refortification of Montségur
1204–7	Cathar/Catholic debates in the Languedoc
1206	March: Dominic de Guzmán proposes preaching in poverty in the Languedoc to bring people back to the Church; the Dominican Order is later founded as a result
1208	14 January: assassination of Peter of Castelnau
	10 March: Innocent calls for a Crusade against the Cathars
1209	18 June: Raymond VI publicly flogged
	22 July: sack of Béziers. At least 9,000 people murdered by Crusaders; start of the Albigensian Crusade
	Early August: siege of Carcassonne

15 August: surrender of Carcassonne
Late August: Simon de Montfort becomes
viscount of Béziers and Carcassonne and
assumes leadership of the Albigensian Crusade
10 November: Raymond Roger Trencavel
found dead in his cell

1210   April: siege and fall of Bram; forced march of
100 blinded and mutilated men to Cabaret;
fall of Cabaret
June/July: siege and fall of Minerve
22 July: 140 Perfect burnt outside Minerve

1211   April/May: siege and fall of Lavaur; 80
knights hanged; Lady Geralda of Lavaur
thrown down a well and stoned to death
3 May: 400 Perfect burnt outside Lavaur
Late May: 50–100 Perfect burnt at Les Cassès

1213   17 January: Innocent suspends the Albigensian
Crusade
21 May: Innocent persuaded to relaunch
Crusade
12 September: Battle of Muret; King Peter II
of Aragon killed; at least 7,000 die with him

1215   20 November: Fourth Lateran Council
transfers land to Simon de Montfort, making
him Lord of all Languedoc

1216   16 July Innocent dies unexpectedly in Perugia
August: sack of Toulouse

1217   13 September: soldiers loyal to Raymond VI
enter Toulouse; siege of Toulouse begins

1218   25 June: Simon de Montfort killed outside

	walls of Toulouse
1219	Massacre of Marmande: 7,000 killed
1221	Death of St Dominic
1222	August: death of Raymond VI
1224	Amaury de Montfort relinquishes control of the Languedoc to the French crown
1225	Death of Arnold Amaury
1226	Spring: Louis VIII's Crusade against the south gets underway
	Cathar Council of Pieusse: bishopric of the Razès founded
	8 November: Louis dies at 39; his widow, Blanche of Castile, becomes Regent
1228	Scorched-earth campaign against Toulouse
1229	12 April: Raymond VII publicly flogged in Paris; end of the Albigensian Crusade
1231	The Inquisition founded to combat Catharism
1233	Spring: Inquisition arrives in the Languedoc
	30 July: first Inquisitor Conrad of Marburg murdered
	August: 200 Cathars and Waldensians burnt in Verona
1234–46	Crusades against heresy in Bosnia
1239	180 heretics burnt at Mont Aimé in Champagne
1240	Trencavel Revolt
1240s	*The Book of the Two Principles* thought to have been written
1242	28 May: Inquisitors Stephen of St Thibéry and William Arnald murdered at Avignonet;

	Raymond VII launches final campaign against the Papacy and French crown
1243	May: siege of Montségur begins
1244	2 March: Montségur surrenders on condition of a two-week truce
	13 March: 21 Believers and mercenaries ask for – and are given – the *Consolamentum*
	16 March: Montségur evacuated; all 225 Perfect are burnt on the so-called Field of the Cremated
1245–46	Extensive Inquisitorial proceedings in the Languedoc
1249	June: Raymond VII burns 80 Cathars at Agen
	September: death of Raymond VII
1252	Inquisitor Peter of Verona (St Peter Martyr) murdered in Italy; use of torture given papal approval by Innocent VI
1255	August: fall of Quéribus, last Cathar stronghold in the Languedoc
1276	Fall of Sirmione, last Cathar fortress in Italy
1278	February: burning of more than 200 Perfect in Verona
1296	October: Peter and William Autier travel to Lombardy to be consoled
1299	Autumn: Autiers return to the Languedoc: start of Cathar revival
1303	Appointment of Geoffrey d'Ablis as Inquisitor in Carcassonne
1305	September: William Bélibaste's first encounter with Autier Perfect while in hiding

	after murdering a fellow shepherd
1307	Appointment of Geoffrey d'Ablis as Inquisitor in Toulouse
	September: Bélibaste, imprisoned for heresy, escapes from jail
1308	8 September: entire village of Montaillou arrested on heresy charges
1309	Late summer: Peter Autier arrested
1310	9 April: Autier burnt at the stake in Toulouse
1315	Bélibaste establishes Cathar community in Morella and Sant Mateu, south of Tarragona in Catalonia
1317	James Fournier becomes bishop of Pamiers and begins Inquisitorial proceedings
1321	March: Bélibaste betrayed and arrested
	Last known Italian Cathar bishop arrested
1325	Pope John XXII calls for action against the Bosnian Church
1329	16 January: Peter Clergue, rector of Montaillou, posthumously burnt
1342	Last known Cathar in Florence appears before the Inquisition
1387–9	Inquisition of Antonio di Settimo di Savigliano. Antonio di Galosna and Jacob Bech arrested and burnt
1412	Posthumous burning of 15 Cathars at Chieri
1459	Bosnian Church persecuted by King Stephen Thomas
1463	Fall of Bosnia to the Ottoman Turks
1867	Last reported Bogomils in Bosnia

Appendix II:
An Heretical Lexicon

A glossary of heresies, heretical practices and other groups mentioned in this book.

Adoptionism Belief that Christ was not born divine, but only became so after his baptism.

Apostolics Sect modelled on the Franciscans. They were founded in 1260 by Gerard Segarelli, and strove to live lives of poverty, humility and service. They believed that the Church had been in decline since the time of Constantine the Great due to its pursuit of power and worldly wealth, and were declared heretical in 1287. Segarelli was burned at Parma in 1300, but the sect continued under the leadership of Brother Dulcin. Jacob Bech, the last known Cathar in the Alps, was a member of the group before converting to Catharism.

Apparellamentum Monthly rite of confession performed by the Perfect, who would usually confess to a Cathar deacon, or, occasionally, a bishop.

Arianism Named after Arius (256–336), a Christian priest from Alexandria, who denied that Christ and God were one person, seeing them instead as two different Divine entities. The heresy was the first serious doctrinal dispute the Church had to face once it had been legalised by Constantine, and it was the major issue faced by the Council of Nicaea.

Believers The majority of Cathars were Believers. That is to say, they had taken the *convenanza*, but were not yet consoled. They were not subject to any dietary restrictions.

Bogomilism Dualist heresy founded by the priest Bogomil in the early tenth century. It appears to have influenced Catharism strongly, although the earliest tangible evidence is only datable to 1167. The movement considerably outlived the Cathars, with reports of Bogomils continuing up to the nineteenth century.

Celtic church According to tradition, the Celtic church was founded by Joseph of Arimathea at Glastonbury during the mid-first century AD, and the case could be made for the Celtic church being the original form of Christianity in Europe. It went into decline after the Synod of Whitby in 664, where it was forcibly absorbed into the Catholic Church. Numerous modern Celtic churches exist today.

Consolamentum Cathar rite of baptism that elevated the Believer to the state of a Perfect. Many Cathars took the *consolamentum* on their deathbeds.

Convenanza Formal rite that made a Cathar Listener a Believer.

Docetism The belief that Christ did not have a physical body, common amongst Gnostics. Docetics believed that Jesus's body was an illusion, as was his crucifixion. Docetism was declared heretical by the Church. Both the Bogomils and the Cathars were Docetist.

Donatism Heresy that denied the validity of offices said by corrupt priests. Many of the reform movements of the eleventh and twelfth centuries were sympathetic to the Donatist position. The Cathars were Donatist in that a *consolamentum* performed by a Perfect who later – even accidentally – broke their vows was invalid.

Dualism The belief that good and evil are two independent, opposing principles. Absolute dualists regard the evil principle to be as strong as the good, and see the two as being locked in conflict for all time. Absolute dualists frequently regard time as cyclical and believe in reincarnation. Moderate dualists see evil as being inferior to the good principle, which will triumph over it at the end of time. Both maintain a hostility to the material world. The Cathars began as moderates, but were converted to absolute Dualism at the Council of St Félix. Some Cathars – such as the Church of Concorezzo – remained moderates.

Elchasaites Jewish Christian sect who were, interestingly, also known as *katharoi*. Their most famous member was the Persian prophet Mani.

Endura Cathar rite that allows the newly consoled nothing but cold water. Mainly associated with the Autier revival – where it was a practical necessity – the *endura* was in fact a feature of Catharism from the beginning.

Essenes Radical Jewish sect that existed from the second century BC to the first century AD. Arguments have been put forward to suggest that both Jesus and John the Baptist had links with the sect. The community at Qumran, which produced the *Dead Sea Scrolls*, is thought to have been Essene.

Gnosticism Term used to designate many different sects who flourished in the first few centuries AD. Although nominally Christian, many elements of Gnosticism are pre-Christian, such as the belief in Dualism. The name derives from the Greek word for knowledge, *gnosis*.

Listeners In the Cathar context, a Listener was a person interested in Catharism, but was not ready or willing to become an actual member of the church, which required the taking of the *convenanza*.

Luciferanism Heresy believed by the Inquisitor Conrad of Marburg to be widespread across Europe. Luciferans were held to worship the devil, engage in orgies and perform child sacrifice. The heresy never actually existed, but that did not stop Pope Gregory IX from issuing the bull *Vox in Rama* in 1233 denouncing it.

Manichaeism Universalist, dualist religion founded by the Persian prophet Mani (216–75). It was seen as the worst heresy since Marcionism (see below), and St Augustine – once a member of the sect – denounced it. It was largely wiped out in Europe during the sixth century, although it survived for another thousand years in Asia. 'Manichaean' became a byword for heretic during the Middle Ages.

Marcionism Gnostic dualist sect that taught the principle of the two gods, with Christ being the son of the true god, and the Jehovah of the Old Testament being seen as the evil god.

Massalianism Dualist heresy that is thought to have originated in fourth-century Mesopotamia. The name means 'the praying people'. Also known as Enthusiasts.

Melioramentum Formal greeting made by a Cathar Believer to a Perfect.

Nestorianism The belief, first proposed by Nestorius (*c*. 386–*c*. 451), the patriarch of Constantinople, that Christ's person contained two separate beings, one human, the other divine. Nestorianism was declared heretical at the Council of Ephesus in 431, but the Nestorian church – despite persecution – survives to this day.

Patarenes Italian name for Cathars. The term was also used in Bosnia.

Paulicianism Dualist heresy that emerged in seventh-century Armenia. In 717, a council of the Armenian Church denounced them as 'sons of Satan' and 'fuel for the fire eternal'. They are thought to have survived until the seventeenth century.

Pelagianism Pelagius (*c.* 360–*c.* 435) was a British monk whose teachings denied Original Sin. Pelagianism was condemned as heresy at the Council of Carthage in 417.

Perfect The Cathar equivalent of priests, they were austere black-robed ascetics who were the heart and soul of the Cathar movement. Bogomilism also had Perfect.

Piphles According to Eckbert of Schönau, this was the name used for dualist heretics in Flanders, although no one knows where the word came from.

Publicans Name used for heretics in the twelfth century, a group of whom came to England to proselytise during the reign of Henry II, probably in the winter of 1165–66.

Simony Strictly speaking, simony is the exchange of something spiritual for something temporal, but it usually refers to the ecclesiastical crime of the buying of offices and privileges by the clergy. Named after Simon Magus, who, in Acts 8.18–24, offers Peter and John money in return for the ability to bestow the Holy Spirit. Dante reserved the Eighth Circle of Hell for simoniacs in the *Inferno.*

Texerant According to Eckbert of Schönau, this was the name used for dualist heretics in France. The name derives from the word for weaving, a craft long associated with heresy.

Waldensians Founded by the preacher Waldo of Lyons (1140–1217), the group espoused evangelical poverty and was also known as the Poor of Lyons as a result. They were declared heretical in the bull *Ad abolendam* in 1184 – which also denounced the Cathars. Despite persecution, the Waldensian church survives to this day.

Suggestions for Further Reading

The most comprehensive book on the Cathars in English is Malcolm Lambert's *The Cathars* (Blackwell, 1998). As a slightly easier read, Malcolm Barber's *The Cathars: Dualist Heretics in Languedoc in the High Middle Ages* (Longman, 2000; second edition 2013) is also recommended. The second edition brings the state of current scholarship up to date.

Stephen O'Shea's *The Perfect Heresy: The Life and Death of the Cathars* (Profile Books, 2000) is perhaps the best non-academic introduction to the Cathars, although the book mainly concentrates on events in the Languedoc (but it does come with copious – and frequently entertaining – endnotes). Italian Catharism is covered by Carol Lansing's *Power & Purity: Cathar Heresy in Medieval Italy* (OUP, 1998).

Late Catharism is most famously represented by Emmanuel Le Roy Ladurie's *Montaillou* (Paris, 1975; English edition, 1980). More recently, René Weis's brilliant *The Yellow Cross: The Story of the Last Cathars 1290–1329* (Penguin, 2001) has covered the same ground in painstaking – and moving – detail.

Older classics on the subject include Sir Steven Runciman's *The Medieval Manichee* (1947) and Zoé Oldenburg's *Massacre at Montségur* (1959).

For actual Cathar texts, the best source remains *Heresies of the High Middle Ages,* edited by Wakefield and Evans (Columbia University Press, 1969).

The two major contemporary accounts of the Albigensian Crusade are *The Song of the Cathar Wars: A History of the Albigensian Crusade* by William of Tudela and an anonymous successor, translated by Janet Shirley (Scolar Press, 1996) and *The History of the Albigensian Crusade: Peter of les Vaux-de-Cernay's Historia Albigensis*, translated by W A and M D Sibly (Boydell, 1998).

In addition to these titles, the curious reader is directed towards the works of Anne Brenon, Jean Duvernoy, Bernard Hamilton and Michel Roquebert, all of whom are major authorities on Catharism.

For the history of Dualism, one should look no further than Yuri Stoyanov's masterly *The Other God* (Yale University Press, 2000), the first edition of which was published as *The Hidden Tradition in Europe* (Penguin, 1994).

With regard to early Christianity, John Davidson's *The Gospel of Jesus: In Search of His Original Teachings* (Element, 1995) is a benchmark in the field, as is Robert Eisenman's *James, the Brother of Jesus* (Faber and Faber, 1997).

The Cathars have been rather ill-served by writers of fiction. Many Cathar novels tend to treat the myths as actual history (which for a novel is, arguably, acceptable), and should be approached with caution. One notable exception is Patrick Harpur's *The Serpent's Circle* (Macmillan, 1985).

Finally, I would like to recommend the works of Arthur Guirdham – the T C Lethbridge of Cathar studies – in particular his *The Cathars and Reincarnation* (Neville Spearman, 1970) and *The Great Heresy: The History and Beliefs of the Cathars* (Neville Spearman, 1977).

And for the adventurous, there is always Chris Ratcliffe and Elaine Connell's *Cycling in Search of the Cathars* (Pennine Pens, 1990).

Select Bibliography

The Cathars

Arnold, John H., *Inquisition and Power: Catharism and the Confessing Subject in Medieval Languedoc* (University of Pennsylvania Press, 2001)

Barber, Malcolm, *The Cathars: Dualist Heretics in Languedoc in the High Middle Ages* (Longman, 2000; second edition, 2013)

Birks, Walter, and Gilbert, R A, *The Treasure of Montségur: A Study of the Cathar Heresy and the Nature of the Cathar Secret* (Crucible, 1987)

Brenon, Anne, *Le Vrai Visage du Catharisme* (Loubatieres, 1988)

_____ , *Les Femmes Cathares* (Perrin, 1992)

Bruschi, Caterina, *The Wandering Heretics of Languedoc* (Cambridge University Press, 2009)

Cartner, George, *Flames of Faith: The Cathars of the Languedoc* (B & C Press, 2003)

Costen, Michael, *The Cathars and the Albigensian Crusade* (Manchester University Press, 1997)

Cowper, Marcus and Dennis, Peter, *Cathar Castles: Fortresses of the Albigensian Crusade, 1209–1300* (Osprey Publishing, 2006)

Dutton, Claire, *Aspects of the Institutional History of the Albigensian Crusades 1198–1229* (Royal Holloway and Bedford New College, University of London, PhD Thesis, 1993)

Duvernoy, Jean, *Le Catharisme* (2 Vols, Privat, 1976/9)

Gordon, James, *The Laity and the Catholic Church in Cathar Languedoc* (Oxford PhD Thesis, 1992)

Guirdham, Arthur, *The Great Heresy: The History and Beliefs of the Cathars* (C W Daniel, 1993)

Hamilton, Bernard, *The Albigensian Crusade* (Historical Association, 1974)

_____ , *Monastic Reform, Catharism and the Crusades 900–1300* (Variorum, 1979)

_____ , *Crusaders, Cathars and the Holy Places* (Ashgate/Variorum, 2000)

Ladurie, Emmanuel Le Roy, *Montaillou* (Penguin, 1980)

Lambert, Malcolm, *The Cathars* (Blackwell, 1998)

Lansing, Carol, *Power & Purity: Cathar Heresy in Medieval Italy* (Oxford University Press, 1998)

Markale, Jean, *Montségur and the Mystery of the Cathars* (Inner Traditions, 2003)

Mundy, John Hine, *The Repression of Catharism at Toulouse: The Royal Diploma of 1279* (Pontifical Institute of Mediaeval Studies, 1985)

_____ , *Men and Women at Toulouse in the Age of the Cathars* (Pontifical Institute of Mediaeval Studies, 1990)

Oldenbourg, Zoé, *Massacre at Montségur: A History of the Albigensian Crusade* (Phoenix, 1998)

O'Shea, Stephen, *The Perfect Heresy: The Revolutionary Life and Death of the Medieval Cathars* (Profile Books, 2000)

_____ , *The Friar of Carcassonne: The Last Days of the Cathars* (Profile Books, 2011)

Pegg, Mark Gregory, *The Corruption of Angels: The Great Inquisition of 1245–1246* (Princeton University Press, 2001)

_____ , *A Most Holy War: The Albigensian Crusade and the Battle for*

Christendom (Oxford University Press, 2008)

Rahn, Otto, *Crusade Against the Grail: The Struggle Between the Cathars, the Templars and the Church of Rome*, Christopher Jones (trans.) (Inner Traditions Bear & Company, 2006)

_____ , *Lucifer's Court: A Heretic's Journey in Search of the Light Bringers*, Christopher Jones (trans.) (Inner Traditions Bear & Company, 2008)

Ratcliffe, Chris, and Connell, Elaine, *Cycling in Search of the Cathars* (Pennine Pens, 1990)

Roach, Andrew, *The Relationship of the Italian and Southern French Cathars, 1170–1320* (University of Oxford, PhD Thesis, 1989)

Roché, Déodat, *Le Catharisme* (Toulouse, 1947)

_____ , *L'Église romaine et les cathares albigeois* (Éditions Cahiers d'études cathares, 1969)

Roquebert, Michel, *L'Epopée cathare* (5 Vols, Privat/Perrin, 1970–98)

Roquette, Yves, *Cathars* (Loubatieres, 1992)

Sumption, Jonathan, *The Albigensian Crusades* (Faber and Faber, 1978)

Strayer, Joseph R, with a new epilogue by Carol Lansing, *The Albigensian Crusades* (University of Michigan Press, 1992)

Taylor, Claire, *Heresy in Medieval France: Dualism in Aquitaine and the Agenais, 1000–1249* (Royal Historical Society/Boydell, 2005)

_____ , *Heresy, Crusade and Inquisition in Medieval Quercy* (York Medieval Press/Boydell & Brewer, 2011)

Wakefield, Walter L., *Heresy, Crusade and Inquisition in Southern France, 1100–1250* (Allen & Unwin, 1974)

Weis, René, *The Yellow Cross: The Story of the Last Cathars, 1290-1329* (Penguin, 2001)

Contemporaneous Accounts and Sources

Hamilton, Janet and Hamilton, Bernard (eds./trans.), with the assistance of Yuri Stoyanov (trans.), *Christian Dualist Heresies in the Byzantine World, c. 650–c. 1450: Selected Sources* (Manchester University Press, 1998)

Léglu, Catherine, Rist, Rebecca and Taylor, Claire (eds.), *The Cathars and the Albigensian Crusade: A Sourcebook*, (Routledge, 2014)

Shirley, Janet (trans.), *The Song of the Cathar Wars: A History of the Albigensian Crusade by William of Tudela and an anonymous successor* (Scolar Press, 1996)

Sibly, W A and Sibly, M D (eds./trans.), *The History of the Albigensian Crusade: Peter of les Vaux-de-Cernay's Historia Albigensis* (Boydell, 1998)

_____ , *The Chronicle of William of Puylaurens: The Albigensian Crusade and its Aftermath* (Boydell & Brewer, 2003)

Wakefield, Walter L. and Evans, Austin P. (eds./trans.), *Heresies of the High Middle Ages* (Columbia University Press, 1991)

Selections from James Fournier's Inquisition proceedings have been translated by Nancy P. Stork and can be viewed online at the website of San José State University, http://www.sjsu.edu/. Search for 'Jacques Fournier' on the home page to find the current location of the pages.

Heresy

Biller, Peter and Hudson, Anne (eds.), *Heresy and Literacy, 1000–1530* (Cambridge University Press, 1994)

Bruschi, Caterina and Biller, Peter (eds), *Texts and the Repression of Medieval Heresy* (York Medieval Press/Boydell & Brewer, 2003)

Fichtenau, Heinrich, *Heretics and Scholars in the High Middle Ages 1000–1200,* Denise A. Kaiser (trans.) (Pennsylvania State University Press, 1998)

Frassetto, Michael, *Heretic Lives: Medieval Heresy from Bogomil and the Cathars to Wyclif and Hus* (Profile Books, 2007)

George, Leonard, *The Encyclopedia of Heresies and Heretics* (Robson Books, 1995)

Lambert, Malcolm, *Medieval Heresy: Popular Movements from the Gregorian Reform to the Reformation* (Blackwell, 2002)

Moore, R I, *The Birth of Popular Heresy* (Edward Arnold, 1975)

————, "Heresy as Disease", in *The Concept of Heresy in the Middle Ages (11th-13th C.),* ed. W. Lourdaux and D. Verhelst (Louvain University Press, 1976)

————, *The War on Heresy: Faith and Power in Medieval Europe* (Profile Books, 2012)

Runciman, Sir Steven, *The Medieval Manichee* (Cambridge University Press, 1947)

Russell, Jeffrey Burton, *Dissent and Reform in the Early Middle Ages* (University of California Press, 1965; reprint: Wipf & Stock, 2005)

Stoyanov, Yuri, *The Other God: Dualist Religions from Antiquity to the Cathar Heresy* (Yale University Press, 2000)

Early Christianity

Baigent, Michael and Leigh, Richard, *The Dead Sea Scrolls Deception* (Arrow Books, 2001)

Davidson, John, *The Gospel of Jesus: In Search of His Original Teachings* (Element, 1995)

Eisenman, Robert, *The Dead Sea Scrolls Uncovered* (with Michael Wise) (Penguin, 1992)

_____, *James, the Brother of Jesus* (Faber, 1997)

Elliott, J K and James, M R (eds.), *The Apocryphal New Testament* (Oxford University Press, 1993)

Kersten, Holger, *Jesus Lived in India* (Element, 1986)

Meyer, Marvin, (ed.), *The Nag Hammadi Scriptures: The Revised and Updated Translation of Sacred Gnostic Texts Complete in One Volume* (HarperCollins, 2007)

Miller, Robert J. (ed.), *The Complete Gospels* (HarperCollins, 1994)

Pagels, Elaine, *The Gnostic Gospels* (Penguin, 1982)

Robinson, James M. (ed.), *The Nag Hammadi Library in English* (HarperCollins, 1990)

Sparks, H F D (ed.), *The Apocryphal Old Testament* (Oxford University Press, 1984)

Vermes, Geza (trans./ed.), *The Complete Dead Sea Scrolls in English* (Penguin, 2004)

Wilson, A N, *Paul: The Mind of the Apostle* (Sinclair-Stevenson, 1997)

Satanology

Pagels, Elaine, *Adam, Eve and the Serpent* (Penguin, 1990)

_____, *The Origin of Satan* (Allen Lane, 1996)

Maxwell-Stuart, P G, *Satan: A Biography* (Amberley Publishing, 2012)

Russell, Jeffrey Burton, *Satan: The Early Christian Tradition*

(Cornell University Press, 1981)

_____ , *Lucifer: The Devil in the Middle Ages* (Cornell University Press, 1984)

Related Interest

Anderson, William, *Dante the Maker* (Routledge & Kegan Paul, 1980)

Angebert, Jean-Michel *The Occult and the Third Reich* (Macmillan, 1974)

Angelov, Dimiter, *The Bogomil Movement* (Sofia Press, 1987)

Armstrong, T J, *Cecilia's Vision* (Headline, 2001)

Baigent, Michael, Leigh, Richard and Lincoln, Henry, *The Holy Blood and the Holy Grail* (Corgi, 1983)

Baigent, Michael and Leigh, Richard, *The Inquisition* (Penguin, 2000)

Barber, Malcolm, *The Two Cities: Medieval Europe, 1050–1320* (Routledge, 1992; second edition, 2004)

Bihalji-Merin, O. and Benac, Alojz, with photographs by Toso Dabac, *The Bogomils* (Thames & Hudson, 1962)

Boyce, Mary, *Zoroastrians: Their Religious Beliefs and Practices* (Routledge & Kegan Paul, 1979)

Clarke, Lindsay, *Parzival and the Stone from Heaven* (Godstow Press, 2011)

Cohn, Norman, *The Pursuit of the Millennium* (Pimlico, 1993)

_____ , *Europe's Inner Demons: The Demonisation of Christians in Medieval Christendom* (Pimlico, 1993)

Fine Jr, J V A, *The Bosnian Church: A New Interpretation* (East European Quarterly, 1975; second edition, Saqi Books, 2007)

Frayling, Christopher, *Strange Landscape: A Journey through the Middle Ages* (Penguin, 1996)

Garsoïan, Nina G., *The Paulician Heresy* (Mouton & Co, 1967; reprint: De Gruyter, 2010)

Ginzburg, Carlo, *The Cheese and the Worms: The Cosmos of a 16th Century Miller* (Penguin, 1992)

Godwin, Malcolm, *The Holy Grail: Its Origins, Secrets & Meaning Revealed* (Bloomsbury, 1994)

Goodrick-Clarke, Nicholas, *The Occult Roots of Nazism* (I B Tauris, 1992)

Guirdham, Arthur, *The Cathars and Reincarnation* (C W Daniel, 1990)

_____ , *We are One Another* (C W Daniel, 1991)

_____ , *The Lake and the Castle* (C W Daniel, 1991)

_____ , *A Foot in Both Worlds* (C W Daniel, 1991)

Hamilton, Bernard, *The Medieval Inquisition* (Edward Arnold, 1981)

Hanratty, Gerald, *Studies in Gnosticism and the Philosophy of Religion* (Four Courts Press, 1997)

Harpur, Patrick, *The Serpent's Circle* (Macmillan, 1985)

Holroyd, Stuart, *The Elements of Gnosticism* (Element, 1994)

Levack, Brian P., *The Witch-Hunt in Early Modern Europe* (Longman, 1995)

Magre, Maurice, *The Return of the Magi,* Reginald Merton (trans.) (Sphere, 1975)

Martin, Lois, *The History of Witchcraft* (Pocket Essentials, 2002; second edition, 2007)

Martin, Sean, *The Knights Templar: The History & Myths of the Legendary Military Order* (Pocket Essentials, 2004; second edition, 2009)

_____ , *The Gnostics: The First Christian Heretics* (Pocket Essentials 2006; second edition, 2010)

Moore, R I, *The Origins of European Dissent* (Blackwell, 1985)

_____ , *The Formation of a Persecuting Society: Power and Deviance in Western Europe, 950–1250* (Blackwell, 1987; second edition, 2007)

Obolensky, Dmitri, *The Bogomils*: A Study in Balkan Neo-Manichaeism (Cambridge University Press, 1948; reprint: Anthony C. Hall, 1972)

Panichas, George (ed.), *The Simone Weil Reader* (Moyer Bell, 1977)

Picknett, Lynne, and Prince, Clive, *The Templar Revelation* (Bantam, 1997)

Richards, Jeffrey, *Sex, Dissidence and Damnation: Minority Groups in the Middle Ages* (Routledge, 1990)

Roszak, Theodore, *Flicker* (No Exit Press, 2005)

Sharenkov, Viktor N., *A Study of Manichaeism in Bulgaria, with special reference to the Bogomils* (New York, 1927)

Tashkovski, Dragan, *Bogomilism in Macedonia* (Macedonian Review Editions, 1975)

Tuchman, Barbara W., *A Distant Mirror: The Calamitous Fourteenth Century* (Macmillan, 1992)

Wolfram von Eschenbach, *Parzival and Titurel*, Cyril Edwards (trans.) (Oxford University Press, 2006)

Index